Service Lines
Complete Self-Assessment Guide

The guidance in this Self-Assessment is ba
practices and standards in business process architecture, design and
quality management. The guidance is also based on the professional
judgment of the individual collaborators listed in the Acknowledgments.

Notice of rights

**You are licensed to use the Self-Assessment contents in your
presentations and materials for internal use and customers
without asking us - we are here to help.**

All rights reserved for the book itself: this book may not be reproduced
or transmitted in any form by any means, electronic, mechanical,
photocopying, recording, or otherwise, without the prior written
permission of the publisher.

The information in this book is distributed on an "As Is" basis without
warranty. While every precaution has been taken in the preparation of he
book, neither the author nor the publisher shall have any liability to any
person or entity with respect to any loss or damage caused or alleged to
be caused directly or indirectly by the instructions contained in this book
or by the products described in it.

Trademarks

Many of the designations used by manufacturers and sellers to
distinguish their products are claimed as trademarks. Where those
designations appear in this book, and the publisher was aware of a
trademark claim, the designations appear as requested by the owner
of the trademark. All other product names and services identified
throughout this book are used in editorial fashion only and for the
benefit of such companies with no intention of infringement of the
trademark. No such use, or the use of any trade name, is intended to
convey endorsement or other affiliation with this book.

Copyright © by The Art of Service
http://theartofservice.com
service@theartofservice.com

Table of Contents

About The Art of Service

The Art of Service, Business Process Architects since 2000, is dedicated to helping stakeholders achieve excellence.

Defining, designing, creating, and implementing a process to solve a stakeholders challenge or meet an objective is the most valuable role… In EVERY group, company, organization and department.

Unless you're talking a one-time, single-use project, there should be a process. Whether that process is managed and implemented by humans, AI, or a combination of the two, it needs to be designed by someone with a complex enough perspective to ask the right questions.

Someone capable of asking the right questions and step back and say, 'What are we really trying to accomplish here? And is there a different way to look at it?'

With The Art of Service's Standard Requirements Self-Assessments, we empower people who can do just that — whether their title is marketer, entrepreneur, manager, salesperson, consultant, Business Process Manager, executive assistant, IT Manager, CIO etc... —they are the people who rule the future. They are people who watch the process as it happens, and ask the right questions to make the process work better.

Contact us when you need any support with this Self-Assessment and any help with templates, blue-prints and examples of standard documents you might need:

http://theartofservice.com
service@theartofservice.com

Acknowledgments

This checklist was developed under the auspices of The Art of Service, chaired by Gerardus Blokdyk.

Representatives from several client companies participated in the preparation of this Self-Assessment.

In addition, we are thankful for the design and printing services provided.

Included Resources - how to access

Included with your purchase of the book is the Service Lines Self-Assessment Spreadsheet Dashboard which contains all questions and Self-Assessment areas and auto-generates insights, graphs, and project RACI planning - all with examples to get you started right away.

How? Simply send an email to
access@theartofservice.com
with this books' title in the subject to get the Service Lines Self Assessment Tool right away.

You will receive the following contents with New and Updated specific criteria:

• The latest quick edition of the book in PDF

• The latest complete edition of the book in PDF, which criteria correspond to the criteria in...

• The Self-Assessment Excel Dashboard, and...

• Example pre-filled Self-Assessment Excel Dashboard to get familiar with results generation

• In-depth specific Checklists covering the topic

• Project management checklists and templates to assist with implementation

INCLUDES LIFETIME SELF ASSESSMENT UPDATES

Every self assessment comes with Lifetime Updates and Lifetime Free Updated Books. Lifetime Updates is an industry-first feature which allows you to receive verified self assessment updates, ensuring you always have the most accurate information at your fingertips.

Get it now- you will be glad you did - do it now, before you forget.

Send an email to **access@theartofservice.com** with this books' title in the subject to get the Service Lines Self Assessment Tool right away.

Your feedback is invaluable to us

If you recently bought this book, we would love to hear from you! You can do this by writing a review on amazon (or the online store where you purchased this book) about your last purchase! As part of our continual service improvement process, we love to hear real client experiences and feedback.

How does it work?
To post a review on Amazon, just log in to your account and click on the Create Your Own Review button (under Customer Reviews) of the relevant product page. You can find examples of product reviews in Amazon. If you purchased from another online store, simply follow their procedures.

What happens when I submit my review?
Once you have submitted your review, send us an email at review@theartofservice.com with the link to your review so we can properly thank you for your feedback.

Purpose of this Self-Assessment

This Self-Assessment has been developed to improve understanding of the requirements and elements of Service Lines, based on best practices and standards in business process architecture, design and quality management.

It is designed to allow for a rapid Self-Assessment to determine how closely existing management practices and procedures correspond to the elements of the Self-Assessment.

The criteria of requirements and elements of Service Lines have been rephrased in the format of a Self-Assessment questionnaire, with a seven-criterion scoring system, as explained in this document.

In this format, even with limited background knowledge of

Service Lines, a manager can quickly review existing operations to determine how they measure up to the standards. This in turn can serve as the starting point of a 'gap analysis' to identify management tools or system elements that might usefully be implemented in the organization to help improve overall performance.

How to use the Self-Assessment

On the following pages are a series of questions to identify to what extent your Service Lines initiative is complete in comparison to the requirements set in standards.

To facilitate answering the questions, there is a space in front of each question to enter a score on a scale of '1' to '5'.

1 Strongly Disagree

2 Disagree

3 Neutral

4 Agree

5 Strongly Agree

Read the question and rate it with the following in front of mind:

'In my belief, the answer to this question is clearly defined'.

There are two ways in which you can choose to interpret this statement;
1. how aware are you that the answer to the question is clearly defined
2. for more in-depth analysis you can choose to gather

evidence and confirm the answer to the question. This obviously will take more time, most Self-Assessment users opt for the first way to interpret the question and dig deeper later on based on the outcome of the overall Self-Assessment.

A score of '1' would mean that the answer is not clear at all, where a '5' would mean the answer is crystal clear and defined. Leave emtpy when the question is not applicable or you don't want to answer it, you can skip it without affecting your score. Write your score in the space provided.

After you have responded to all the appropriate statements in each section, compute your average score for that section, using the formula provided, and round to the nearest tenth. Then transfer to the corresponding spoke in the Service Lines Scorecard on the second next page of the Self-Assessment.

Your completed Service Lines Scorecard will give you a clear presentation of which Service Lines areas need attention.

Service Lines
Scorecard Example

Example of how the finalized Scorecard can look like:

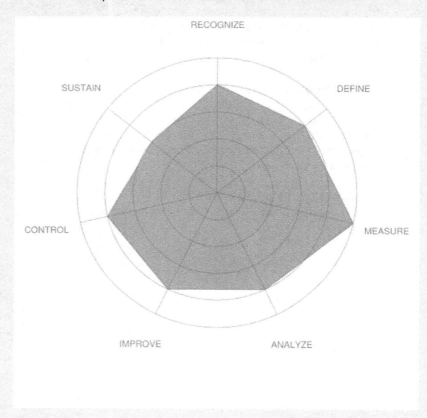

Service Lines
Scorecard

Your Scores:

BEGINNING OF THE SELF-ASSESSMENT:

CRITERION #1: RECOGNIZE

INTENT: Be aware of the need for change. Recognize that there is an unfavorable variation, problem or symptom.

In my belief, the answer to this question is clearly defined:

5 Strongly Agree

4 Agree

3 Neutral

2 Disagree

1 Strongly Disagree

1. Does the problem have ethical dimensions?
<--- Score

2. How do you recognize an Service Lines objection?
<--- Score

3. Are there recognized Service Lines problems?
<--- Score

4. What activities does the governance board need to consider?
<--- Score

5. Who are your key stakeholders who need to sign off?
<--- Score

6. Who needs what information?
<--- Score

7. Are there any specific expectations or concerns about the Service Lines team, Service Lines itself?
<--- Score

8. Who defines the rules in relation to any given issue?
<--- Score

9. Did you miss any major Service Lines issues?
<--- Score

10. For your Service Lines project, identify and describe the business environment, is there more than one layer to the business environment?
<--- Score

11. What else needs to be measured?
<--- Score

12. Do you recognize Service Lines achievements?
<--- Score

13. Are employees recognized for desired behaviors?
<--- Score

14. How are training requirements identified?

<--- Score

15. What information do users need?
<--- Score

16. How do you recognize an objection?
<--- Score

17. What is the Service Lines problem definition? What do you need to resolve?
<--- Score

18. Which needs are not included or involved?
<--- Score

19. What creative shifts do you need to take?
<--- Score

20. Looking at each person individually – does every one have the qualities which are needed to work in this group?
<--- Score

21. How many trainings, in total, are needed?
<--- Score

22. What training and capacity building actions are needed to implement proposed reforms?
<--- Score

23. What are the timeframes required to resolve each of the issues/problems?
<--- Score

24. Is the need for organizational change recognized?
<--- Score

25. How do you identify subcontractor relationships?
<--- Score

26. What prevents you from making the changes you know will make you a more effective Service Lines leader?
<--- Score

27. What does Service Lines success mean to the stakeholders?
<--- Score

28. Which information does the Service Lines business case need to include?
<--- Score

29. How does it fit into your organizational needs and tasks?
<--- Score

30. What tools and technologies are needed for a custom Service Lines project?
<--- Score

31. Are losses recognized in a timely manner?
<--- Score

32. Have you identified your Service Lines key performance indicators?
<--- Score

33. What are the stakeholder objectives to be achieved with Service Lines?
<--- Score

34. Are there regulatory / compliance issues?
<--- Score

35. What is the problem and/or vulnerability?
<--- Score

36. Do you need different information or graphics?
<--- Score

37. To what extent would your organization benefit from being recognized as a award recipient?
<--- Score

38. Do you know what you need to know about Service Lines?
<--- Score

39. What should be considered when identifying available resources, constraints, and deadlines?
<--- Score

40. What is the extent or complexity of the Service Lines problem?
<--- Score

41. What is the problem or issue?
<--- Score

42. What Service Lines problem should be solved?
<--- Score

43. Consider your own Service Lines project, what types of organizational problems do you think might be causing or affecting your problem, based on the work done so far?
<--- Score

44. Where is training needed?
<--- Score

45. Whom do you really need or want to serve?
<--- Score

46. What situation(s) led to this Service Lines Self Assessment?
<--- Score

47. What is the smallest subset of the problem you can usefully solve?
<--- Score

48. Is the quality assurance team identified?
<--- Score

49. How are you going to measure success?
<--- Score

50. As a sponsor, customer or management, how important is it to meet goals, objectives?
<--- Score

51. Why the need?
<--- Score

52. Will Service Lines deliverables need to be tested and, if so, by whom?
<--- Score

53. Will it solve real problems?
<--- Score

54. What do employees need in the short term?

<--- Score

55. Are employees recognized or rewarded for performance that demonstrates the highest levels of integrity?
<--- Score

56. Are your goals realistic? Do you need to redefine your problem? Perhaps the problem has changed or maybe you have reached your goal and need to set a new one?
<--- Score

57. How much are sponsors, customers, partners, stakeholders involved in Service Lines? In other words, what are the risks, if Service Lines does not deliver successfully?
<--- Score

58. Who needs to know about Service Lines?
<--- Score

59. Are controls defined to recognize and contain problems?
<--- Score

60. What needs to be done?
<--- Score

61. Are there any revenue recognition issues?
<--- Score

62. What vendors make products that address the Service Lines needs?
<--- Score

63. Is it clear when you think of the day ahead of you what activities and tasks you need to complete?
<--- Score

64. How can auditing be a preventative security measure?
<--- Score

65. What needs to stay?
<--- Score

66. To what extent does each concerned units management team recognize Service Lines as an effective investment?
<--- Score

67. When a Service Lines manager recognizes a problem, what options are available?
<--- Score

68. What Service Lines events should you attend?
<--- Score

69. What resources or support might you need?
<--- Score

70. Are you dealing with any of the same issues today as yesterday? What can you do about this?
<--- Score

71. What are the Service Lines resources needed?
<--- Score

72. Does your organization need more Service Lines education?
<--- Score

73. What would happen if Service Lines weren't done?
<--- Score

74. What are the expected benefits of Service Lines to the stakeholder?
<--- Score

75. How are the Service Lines's objectives aligned to the group's overall stakeholder strategy?
<--- Score

76. Do you need to avoid or amend any Service Lines activities?
<--- Score

77. Who needs to know?
<--- Score

78. Is it needed?
<--- Score

79. How do you take a forward-looking perspective in identifying Service Lines research related to market response and models?
<--- Score

80. Why is this needed?
<--- Score

81. Will new equipment/products be required to facilitate Service Lines delivery, for example is new software needed?
<--- Score

82. What are the minority interests and what amount

of minority interests can be recognized?
<--- Score

83. Who needs budgets?
<--- Score

84. What are your needs in relation to Service Lines
skills, labor, equipment, and markets?
<--- Score

85. Are there Service Lines problems defined?
<--- Score

86. What problems are you facing and how do
you consider Service Lines will circumvent those
obstacles?
<--- Score

87. Who else hopes to benefit from it?
<--- Score

88. What Service Lines coordination do you need?
<--- Score

89. Who should resolve the Service Lines issues?
<--- Score

90. How do you identify the kinds of information that
you will need?
<--- Score

91. Are problem definition and motivation clearly
presented?
<--- Score

92. Will a response program recognize when a crisis

occurs and provide some level of response?
<--- Score

93. Can management personnel recognize the monetary benefit of Service Lines?
<--- Score

94. Does Service Lines create potential expectations in other areas that need to be recognized and considered?
<--- Score

95. What is the recognized need?
<--- Score

96. What are the clients issues and concerns?
<--- Score

97. What do you need to start doing?
<--- Score

98. Which issues are too important to ignore?
<--- Score

Add up total points for this section:
_ _ _ _ _ = Total points for this section

Divided by: _ _ _ _ _ _ (number of statements answered) = _ _ _ _ _ _
Average score for this section

Transfer your score to the Service Lines Index at the beginning of the Self-Assessment.

CRITERION #2: DEFINE:

INTENT: Formulate the stakeholder problem. Define the problem, needs and objectives.

In my belief, the answer to this question is clearly defined:

5 Strongly Agree

4 Agree

3 Neutral

2 Disagree

1 Strongly Disagree

1. Is the team sponsored by a champion or stakeholder leader?
<--- Score

2. How do you gather requirements?
<--- Score

3. What information should you gather?
<--- Score

4. Who defines (or who defined) the rules and roles?
<--- Score

5. Are there any constraints known that bear on the ability to perform Service Lines work? How is the team addressing them?
<--- Score

6. Are customer(s) identified and segmented according to their different needs and requirements?
<--- Score

7. What intelligence can you gather?
<--- Score

8. What Service Lines services do you require?
<--- Score

9. What scope to assess?
<--- Score

10. Who are the Service Lines improvement team members, including Management Leads and Coaches?
<--- Score

11. How do you catch Service Lines definition inconsistencies?
<--- Score

12. What Service Lines requirements should be gathered?
<--- Score

13. How do you manage scope?

<--- Score

14. Is the work to date meeting requirements?
<--- Score

15. Are audit criteria, scope, frequency and methods defined?
<--- Score

16. Has a team charter been developed and communicated?
<--- Score

17. Do you have organizational privacy requirements?
<--- Score

18. What system do you use for gathering Service Lines information?
<--- Score

19. Do you all define Service Lines in the same way?
<--- Score

20. How often are the team meetings?
<--- Score

21. What is the worst case scenario?
<--- Score

22. What defines best in class?
<--- Score

23. Is the Service Lines scope manageable?
<--- Score

24. Is there a completed SIPOC representation,

describing the Suppliers, Inputs, Process, Outputs, and Customers?
<--- Score

25. What constraints exist that might impact the team?
<--- Score

26. Is scope creep really all bad news?
<--- Score

27. How and when will the baselines be defined?
<--- Score

28. Have all basic functions of Service Lines been defined?
<--- Score

29. What information do you gather?
<--- Score

30. Who is gathering information?
<--- Score

31. What key stakeholder process output measure(s) does Service Lines leverage and how?
<--- Score

32. What is the definition of Service Lines excellence?
<--- Score

33. What knowledge or experience is required?
<--- Score

34. When are meeting minutes sent out? Who is on the distribution list?

<--- Score

35. When is/was the Service Lines start date?
<--- Score

36. How would you define the culture at your organization, how susceptible is it to Service Lines changes?
<--- Score

37. How does the Service Lines manager ensure against scope creep?
<--- Score

38. Are improvement team members fully trained on Service Lines?
<--- Score

39. Is there regularly 100% attendance at the team meetings? If not, have appointed substitutes attended to preserve cross-functionality and full representation?
<--- Score

40. What are the boundaries of the scope? What is in bounds and what is not? What is the start point? What is the stop point?
<--- Score

41. Are the Service Lines requirements complete?
<--- Score

42. What is the scope?
<--- Score

43. Are stakeholder processes mapped?

<--- Score

44. What are the compelling stakeholder reasons for embarking on Service Lines?
<--- Score

45. What is out of scope?
<--- Score

46. How will variation in the actual durations of each activity be dealt with to ensure that the expected Service Lines results are met?
<--- Score

47. What is the definition of success?
<--- Score

48. What are the Service Lines tasks and definitions?
<--- Score

49. In what way can you redefine the criteria of choice clients have in your category in your favor?
<--- Score

50. If substitutes have been appointed, have they been briefed on the Service Lines goals and received regular communications as to the progress to date?
<--- Score

51. What are (control) requirements for Service Lines Information?
<--- Score

52. What are the core elements of the Service Lines business case?
<--- Score

53. Has a high-level 'as is' process map been completed, verified and validated?
<--- Score

54. Is there a clear Service Lines case definition?
<--- Score

55. How do you hand over Service Lines context?
<--- Score

56. What would be the goal or target for a Service Lines's improvement team?
<--- Score

57. How is the team tracking and documenting its work?
<--- Score

58. How would you define Service Lines leadership?
<--- Score

59. What gets examined?
<--- Score

60. What are the Roles and Responsibilities for each team member and its leadership? Where is this documented?
<--- Score

61. Who is gathering Service Lines information?
<--- Score

62. Are different versions of process maps needed to account for the different types of inputs?
<--- Score

63. Has/have the customer(s) been identified?
<--- Score

64. What are the tasks and definitions?
<--- Score

65. What is out-of-scope initially?
<--- Score

66. How do you manage changes in Service Lines requirements?
<--- Score

67. Is there a critical path to deliver Service Lines results?
<--- Score

68. Are task requirements clearly defined?
<--- Score

69. Who approved the Service Lines scope?
<--- Score

70. What is the scope of Service Lines?
<--- Score

71. What is the scope of the Service Lines work?
<--- Score

72. Are required metrics defined, what are they?
<--- Score

73. How do you manage unclear Service Lines requirements?
<--- Score

74. Have all of the relationships been defined properly?
<--- Score

75. Is the scope of Service Lines defined?
<--- Score

76. Why are you doing Service Lines and what is the scope?
<--- Score

77. Are roles and responsibilities formally defined?
<--- Score

78. What baselines are required to be defined and managed?
<--- Score

79. How did the Service Lines manager receive input to the development of a Service Lines improvement plan and the estimated completion dates/times of each activity?
<--- Score

80. What is in the scope and what is not in scope?
<--- Score

81. Has anyone else (internal or external to the group) attempted to solve this problem or a similar one before? If so, what knowledge can be leveraged from these previous efforts?
<--- Score

82. How was the 'as is' process map developed, reviewed, verified and validated?

<--- Score

83. What is in scope?
<--- Score

84. Has everyone on the team, including the team leaders, been properly trained?
<--- Score

85. How will the Service Lines team and the group measure complete success of Service Lines?
<--- Score

86. Has a project plan, Gantt chart, or similar been developed/completed?
<--- Score

87. Has a Service Lines requirement not been met?
<--- Score

88. What was the context?
<--- Score

89. Is the team adequately staffed with the desired cross-functionality? If not, what additional resources are available to the team?
<--- Score

90. The political context: who holds power?
<--- Score

91. Are there different segments of customers?
<--- Score

92. Are team charters developed?
<--- Score

93. Is special Service Lines user knowledge required?
<--- Score

94. Is Service Lines currently on schedule according to the plan?
<--- Score

95. Has the Service Lines work been fairly and/ or equitably divided and delegated among team members who are qualified and capable to perform the work? Has everyone contributed?
<--- Score

96. Has the improvement team collected the 'voice of the customer' (obtained feedback – qualitative and quantitative)?
<--- Score

97. Are accountability and ownership for Service Lines clearly defined?
<--- Score

98. What sources do you use to gather information for a Service Lines study?
<--- Score

99. Does the team have regular meetings?
<--- Score

100. How do you keep key subject matter experts in the loop?
<--- Score

101. Do the problem and goal statements meet the SMART criteria (specific, measurable, attainable,

relevant, and time-bound)?
<--- Score

102. Will a Service Lines production readiness review be required?
<--- Score

103. Is there a completed, verified, and validated high-level 'as is' (not 'should be' or 'could be') stakeholder process map?
<--- Score

104. Does the scope remain the same?
<--- Score

105. What is the scope of the Service Lines effort?
<--- Score

106. Are resources adequate for the scope?
<--- Score

107. What specifically is the problem? Where does it occur? When does it occur? What is its extent?
<--- Score

108. Are all requirements met?
<--- Score

109. What is a worst-case scenario for losses?
<--- Score

110. Is data collected and displayed to better understand customer(s) critical needs and requirements.
<--- Score

111. Have the customer needs been translated into specific, measurable requirements? How?
<--- Score

112. Will team members perform Service Lines work when assigned and in a timely fashion?
<--- Score

113. How do you gather Service Lines requirements?
<--- Score

114. Is the team equipped with available and reliable resources?
<--- Score

115. Is it clearly defined in and to your organization what you do?
<--- Score

116. What sort of initial information to gather?
<--- Score

117. What are the dynamics of the communication plan?
<--- Score

118. When is the estimated completion date?
<--- Score

119. Is the improvement team aware of the different versions of a process: what they think it is vs. what it actually is vs. what it should be vs. what it could be?
<--- Score

120. Is full participation by members in regularly held team meetings guaranteed?

<--- Score

121. Is the team formed and are team leaders (Coaches and Management Leads) assigned?
<--- Score

122. Is Service Lines linked to key stakeholder goals and objectives?
<--- Score

123. What are the record-keeping requirements of Service Lines activities?
<--- Score

124. Is the current 'as is' process being followed? If not, what are the discrepancies?
<--- Score

125. Is there a Service Lines management charter, including stakeholder case, problem and goal statements, scope, milestones, roles and responsibilities, communication plan?
<--- Score

126. Has your scope been defined?
<--- Score

127. What are the Service Lines use cases?
<--- Score

128. How do you gather the stories?
<--- Score

129. What is the context?
<--- Score

130. Are the Service Lines requirements testable?
<--- Score

131. What critical content must be communicated –
who, what, when, where, and how?
<--- Score

132. How can the value of Service Lines be defined?
<--- Score

133. How have you defined all Service Lines
requirements first?
<--- Score

134. What are the requirements for audit information?
<--- Score

135. Will team members regularly document their
Service Lines work?
<--- Score

136. What are the rough order estimates on cost
savings/opportunities that Service Lines brings?
<--- Score

137. Has the direction changed at all during the
course of Service Lines? If so, when did it change and
why?
<--- Score

138. What customer feedback methods were used to
solicit their input?
<--- Score

139. What scope do you want your strategy to cover?
<--- Score

140. Is there any additional Service Lines definition of success?
<--- Score

Add up total points for this section:
_____ = Total points for this section

Divided by: _____ (number of statements answered) = _____
Average score for this section

Transfer your score to the Service Lines Index at the beginning of the Self-Assessment.

CRITERION #3: MEASURE:

INTENT: Gather the correct data.
Measure the current performance and
evolution of the situation.

In my belief, the answer to this
question is clearly defined:

5 Strongly Agree

4 Agree

3 Neutral

2 Disagree

1 Strongly Disagree

1. Does a Service Lines quantification method exist?
<--- Score

2. How are costs allocated?
<--- Score

3. What are the Service Lines key cost drivers?
<--- Score

4. How do you verify your resources?
<--- Score

5. What are your key Service Lines organizational performance measures, including key short and longer-term financial measures?
<--- Score

6. What is the cost of rework?
<--- Score

7. What causes investor action?
<--- Score

8. How do you control the overall costs of your work processes?
<--- Score

9. What is your Service Lines quality cost segregation study?
<--- Score

10. How do you verify and develop ideas and innovations?
<--- Score

11. Have design-to-cost goals been established?
<--- Score

12. What are the costs of reform?
<--- Score

13. Do you aggressively reward and promote the people who have the biggest impact on creating excellent Service Lines services/products?
<--- Score

14. Are the Service Lines benefits worth its costs?
<--- Score

15. What can be used to verify compliance?
<--- Score

16. How can you reduce costs?
<--- Score

17. How do you measure variability?
<--- Score

18. Are you taking your company in the direction of better and revenue or cheaper and cost?
<--- Score

19. What are the costs of delaying Service Lines action?
<--- Score

20. Have you included everything in your Service Lines cost models?
<--- Score

21. What are the operational costs after Service Lines deployment?
<--- Score

22. What are hidden Service Lines quality costs?
<--- Score

23. How can a Service Lines test verify your ideas or assumptions?
<--- Score

24. How will measures be used to manage and adapt?
<--- Score

25. What would it cost to replace your technology?
<--- Score

26. Are actual costs in line with budgeted costs?
<--- Score

27. How will you measure your Service Lines effectiveness?
<--- Score

28. How do you measure efficient delivery of Service Lines services?
<--- Score

29. What is the total cost related to deploying Service Lines, including any consulting or professional services?
<--- Score

30. Do you have a flow diagram of what happens?
<--- Score

31. Where is the cost?
<--- Score

32. Which measures and indicators matter?
<--- Score

33. How long to keep data and how to manage retention costs?
<--- Score

34. What evidence is there and what is measured?

<--- Score

35. Will Service Lines have an impact on current business continuity, disaster recovery processes and/or infrastructure?
<--- Score

36. Are indirect costs charged to the Service Lines program?
<--- Score

37. What happens if cost savings do not materialize?
<--- Score

38. Are there competing Service Lines priorities?
<--- Score

39. When should you bother with diagrams?
<--- Score

40. What users will be impacted?
<--- Score

41. When are costs are incurred?
<--- Score

42. What does losing customers cost your organization?
<--- Score

43. How do you verify the authenticity of the data and information used?
<--- Score

44. What could cause you to change course?
<--- Score

45. Which Service Lines impacts are significant?
<--- Score

46. How to cause the change?
<--- Score

47. How frequently do you track Service Lines measures?
<--- Score

48. Do the benefits outweigh the costs?
<--- Score

49. What are your operating costs?
<--- Score

50. Did you tackle the cause or the symptom?
<--- Score

51. Where is it measured?
<--- Score

52. What is the Service Lines business impact?
<--- Score

53. Who should receive measurement reports?
<--- Score

54. What relevant entities could be measured?
<--- Score

55. How do you measure lifecycle phases?
<--- Score

56. Have you made assumptions about the shape of

the future, particularly its impact on your customers and competitors?
<--- Score

57. Are Service Lines vulnerabilities categorized and prioritized?
<--- Score

58. Does management have the right priorities among projects?
<--- Score

59. How can you measure Service Lines in a systematic way?
<--- Score

60. Why do you expend time and effort to implement measurement, for whom?
<--- Score

61. What is the total fixed cost?
<--- Score

62. Do you have any cost Service Lines limitation requirements?
<--- Score

63. What drives O&M cost?
<--- Score

64. Has a cost center been established?
<--- Score

65. How can you reduce the costs of obtaining inputs?
<--- Score

66. Are the measurements objective?
<--- Score

67. What are your primary costs, revenues, assets?
<--- Score

68. What does a Test Case verify?
<--- Score

69. How do you prevent mis-estimating cost?
<--- Score

70. How sensitive must the Service Lines strategy be to cost?
<--- Score

71. How do you verify the Service Lines requirements quality?
<--- Score

72. How will success or failure be measured?
<--- Score

73. Are you able to realize any cost savings?
<--- Score

74. What tests verify requirements?
<--- Score

75. What is an unallowable cost?
<--- Score

76. How do you verify performance?
<--- Score

77. What are the costs?

<--- Score

78. What is the root cause(s) of the problem?
<--- Score

79. How are measurements made?
<--- Score

80. How do your measurements capture actionable Service Lines information for use in exceeding your customers expectations and securing your customers engagement?
<--- Score

81. What are the uncertainties surrounding estimates of impact?
<--- Score

82. What measurements are possible, practicable and meaningful?
<--- Score

83. What details are required of the Service Lines cost structure?
<--- Score

84. What are the Service Lines investment costs?
<--- Score

85. Is it possible to estimate the impact of unanticipated complexity such as wrong or failed assumptions, feedback, etcetera on proposed reforms?
<--- Score

86. At what cost?

<--- Score

87. What are your customers expectations and measures?
<--- Score

88. How is performance measured?
<--- Score

89. How do you quantify and qualify impacts?
<--- Score

90. What do you measure and why?
<--- Score

91. How do you aggregate measures across priorities?
<--- Score

92. What methods are feasible and acceptable to estimate the impact of reforms?
<--- Score

93. Among the Service Lines product and service cost to be estimated, which is considered hardest to estimate?
<--- Score

94. What is your decision requirements diagram?
<--- Score

95. Who pays the cost?
<--- Score

96. Why do the measurements/indicators matter?
<--- Score

97. How will costs be allocated?
<--- Score

98. What would be a real cause for concern?
<--- Score

99. What does your operating model cost?
<--- Score

100. Are you aware of what could cause a problem?
<--- Score

101. When a disaster occurs, who gets priority?
<--- Score

102. What disadvantage does this cause for the user?
<--- Score

103. What are the strategic priorities for this year?
<--- Score

104. What causes extra work or rework?
<--- Score

105. Is the cost worth the Service Lines effort ?
<--- Score

106. Are there measurements based on task performance?
<--- Score

107. How will your organization measure success?
<--- Score

108. What are the costs and benefits?
<--- Score

109. What is measured? Why?
<--- Score

110. How is the value delivered by Service Lines being measured?
<--- Score

111. What are the types and number of measures to use?
<--- Score

112. Are the units of measure consistent?
<--- Score

113. Is there an opportunity to verify requirements?
<--- Score

114. What is the cause of any Service Lines gaps?
<--- Score

115. Do you effectively measure and reward individual and team performance?
<--- Score

116. How will effects be measured?
<--- Score

117. Does the Service Lines task fit the client's priorities?
<--- Score

118. What causes innovation to fail or succeed in your organization?
<--- Score

119. How can you measure the performance?
<--- Score

120. What could cause delays in the schedule?
<--- Score

121. What are allowable costs?
<--- Score

122. What do people want to verify?
<--- Score

123. What harm might be caused?
<--- Score

124. How will you measure success?
<--- Score

125. How can you manage cost down?
<--- Score

126. What potential environmental factors impact the Service Lines effort?
<--- Score

127. How do you verify if Service Lines is built right?
<--- Score

128. Are missed Service Lines opportunities costing your organization money?
<--- Score

129. Is the solution cost-effective?
<--- Score

130. How do you measure success?

<--- Score

131. How is progress measured?
<--- Score

Add up total points for this section:
_____ = Total points for this section

Divided by: _____ (number of
statements answered) = _____
Average score for this section

Transfer your score to the Service Lines
Index at the beginning of the Self-
Assessment.

CRITERION #4: ANALYZE:

INTENT: Analyze causes, assumptions and hypotheses.

In my belief, the answer to this question is clearly defined:

5 Strongly Agree

4 Agree

3 Neutral

2 Disagree

1 Strongly Disagree

1. How is the way you as the leader think and process information affecting your organizational culture?
<--- Score

2. What types of data do your Service Lines indicators require?
<--- Score

3. What quality tools were used to get through the analyze phase?

<--- Score

4. What successful thing are you doing today that may be blinding you to new growth opportunities?
<--- Score

5. Who qualifies to gain access to data?
<--- Score

6. How are outputs preserved and protected?
<--- Score

7. What data do you need to collect?
<--- Score

8. Do you understand your management processes today?
<--- Score

9. Have the problem and goal statements been updated to reflect the additional knowledge gained from the analyze phase?
<--- Score

10. How do mission and objectives affect the Service Lines processes of your organization?
<--- Score

11. How will corresponding data be collected?
<--- Score

12. What other jobs or tasks affect the performance of the steps in the Service Lines process?
<--- Score

13. What Service Lines data should be collected?

<--- Score

14. Were any designed experiments used to generate additional insight into the data analysis?
<--- Score

15. What information qualified as important?
<--- Score

16. Do quality systems drive continuous improvement?
<--- Score

17. How is the data gathered?
<--- Score

18. How has the Service Lines data been gathered?
<--- Score

19. What, related to, Service Lines processes does your organization outsource?
<--- Score

20. How do you measure the operational performance of your key work systems and processes, including productivity, cycle time, and other appropriate measures of process effectiveness, efficiency, and innovation?
<--- Score

21. Do staff qualifications match your project?
<--- Score

22. Are all staff in core Service Lines subjects Highly Qualified?
<--- Score

23. What qualifications are needed?
<--- Score

24. How do you use Service Lines data and information to support organizational decision making and innovation?
<--- Score

25. What process should you select for improvement?
<--- Score

26. What conclusions were drawn from the team's data collection and analysis? How did the team reach these conclusions?
<--- Score

27. How will the Service Lines data be captured?
<--- Score

28. What are the best opportunities for value improvement?
<--- Score

29. What Service Lines metrics are outputs of the process?
<--- Score

30. What Service Lines data should be managed?
<--- Score

31. Was a detailed process map created to amplify critical steps of the 'as is' stakeholder process?
<--- Score

32. Where is Service Lines data gathered?

<--- Score

33. Who will facilitate the team and process?
<--- Score

34. Who gets your output?
<--- Score

35. What kind of crime could a potential new hire
have committed that would not only not disqualify
him/her from being hired by your organization,
but would actually indicate that he/she might be a
particularly good fit?
<--- Score

36. What Service Lines data do you gather or use now?
<--- Score

37. Are your outputs consistent?
<--- Score

38. Is the Service Lines process severely broken such
that a re-design is necessary?
<--- Score

39. Was a cause-and-effect diagram used to explore
the different types of causes (or sources of variation)?
<--- Score

40. Has an output goal been set?
<--- Score

41. Are Service Lines changes recognized early
enough to be approved through the regular process?
<--- Score

42. Did any value-added analysis or 'lean thinking' take place to identify some of the gaps shown on the 'as is' process map?
<--- Score

43. Who owns what data?
<--- Score

44. Have any additional benefits been identified that will result from closing all or most of the gaps?
<--- Score

45. Do you, as a leader, bounce back quickly from setbacks?
<--- Score

46. What methods do you use to gather Service Lines data?
<--- Score

47. What does the data say about the performance of the stakeholder process?
<--- Score

48. What are the Service Lines business drivers?
<--- Score

49. Is the performance gap determined?
<--- Score

50. What do you need to qualify?
<--- Score

51. Record-keeping requirements flow from the records needed as inputs, outputs, controls and for transformation of a Service Lines process, are the

records needed as inputs to the Service Lines process available?
<--- Score

52. Is the final output clearly identified?
<--- Score

53. What are your outputs?
<--- Score

54. How do you identify specific Service Lines investment opportunities and emerging trends?
<--- Score

55. Who will gather what data?
<--- Score

56. Is the suppliers process defined and controlled?
<--- Score

57. Who is involved in the management review process?
<--- Score

58. Identify an operational issue in your organization, for example, could a particular task be done more quickly or more efficiently by Service Lines?
<--- Score

59. What are the processes for audit reporting and management?
<--- Score

60. What process improvements will be needed?
<--- Score

61. How will the data be checked for quality?
<--- Score

62. How is data used for program management and improvement?
<--- Score

63. What is the output?
<--- Score

64. What is the Service Lines Driver?
<--- Score

65. Have you defined which data is gathered how?
<--- Score

66. Do your contracts/agreements contain data security obligations?
<--- Score

67. Can you add value to the current Service Lines decision-making process (largely qualitative) by incorporating uncertainty modeling (more quantitative)?
<--- Score

68. Has data output been validated?
<--- Score

69. What did the team gain from developing a sub-process map?
<--- Score

70. Is there an established change management process?
<--- Score

71. What are the Service Lines design outputs?
<--- Score

72. What were the financial benefits resulting from any 'ground fruit or low-hanging fruit' (quick fixes)?
<--- Score

73. What internal processes need improvement?
<--- Score

74. What are your current levels and trends in key measures or indicators of Service Lines product and process performance that are important to and directly serve your customers? How do these results compare with the performance of your competitors and other organizations with similar offerings?
<--- Score

75. Is data and process analysis, root cause analysis and quantifying the gap/opportunity in place?
<--- Score

76. How do you implement and manage your work processes to ensure that they meet design requirements?
<--- Score

77. Where can you get qualified talent today?
<--- Score

78. What is the Value Stream Mapping?
<--- Score

79. What are your best practices for minimizing Service Lines project risk, while demonstrating

incremental value and quick wins throughout the Service Lines project lifecycle?

<--- Score

80. What output to create?

<--- Score

81. Which Service Lines data should be retained?

<--- Score

82. What is the oversight process?

<--- Score

83. Who is involved with workflow mapping?

<--- Score

84. Were there any improvement opportunities identified from the process analysis?

<--- Score

85. How does the organization define, manage, and improve its Service Lines processes?

<--- Score

86. What are the necessary qualifications?

<--- Score

87. How is Service Lines data gathered?

<--- Score

88. How do you ensure that the Service Lines opportunity is realistic?

<--- Score

89. What is your organizations system for selecting qualified vendors?

<--- Score

90. How often will data be collected for measures?
<--- Score

91. What were the crucial 'moments of truth' on the process map?
<--- Score

92. Are all team members qualified for all tasks?
<--- Score

93. What qualifications do Service Lines leaders need?
<--- Score

94. Should you invest in industry-recognized qualifications?
<--- Score

95. What are the revised rough estimates of the financial savings/opportunity for Service Lines improvements?
<--- Score

96. What are evaluation criteria for the output?
<--- Score

97. How difficult is it to qualify what Service Lines ROI is?
<--- Score

98. How many input/output points does it require?
<--- Score

99. What are the disruptive Service Lines technologies that enable your organization to radically change your

business processes?
<--- Score

100. What is your organizations process which leads to recognition of value generation?
<--- Score

101. How much data can be collected in the given timeframe?
<--- Score

102. Is the gap/opportunity displayed and communicated in financial terms?
<--- Score

103. What is the complexity of the output produced?
<--- Score

104. What systems/processes must you excel at?
<--- Score

105. What Service Lines data will be collected?
<--- Score

106. Do you have the authority to produce the output?
<--- Score

107. What tools were used to generate the list of possible causes?
<--- Score

108. Is there any way to speed up the process?
<--- Score

109. How do you define collaboration and team

output?
<--- Score

110. When should a process be art not science?
<--- Score

111. Are you missing Service Lines opportunities?
<--- Score

112. Is pre-qualification of suppliers carried out?
<--- Score

113. How is the Service Lines Value Stream Mapping managed?
<--- Score

114. How was the detailed process map generated, verified, and validated?
<--- Score

115. What are your Service Lines processes?
<--- Score

116. What other organizational variables, such as reward systems or communication systems, affect the performance of this Service Lines process?
<--- Score

117. Is there a strict change management process?
<--- Score

118. What training and qualifications will you need?
<--- Score

119. What are your current levels and trends in key Service Lines measures or indicators of product

and process performance that are important to and directly serve your customers?
<--- Score

120. A compounding model resolution with available relevant data can often provide insight towards a solution methodology; which Service Lines models, tools and techniques are necessary?
<--- Score

121. What are the personnel training and qualifications required?
<--- Score

122. Do your leaders quickly bounce back from setbacks?
<--- Score

123. What controls do you have in place to protect data?
<--- Score

124. Were Pareto charts (or similar) used to portray the 'heavy hitters' (or key sources of variation)?
<--- Score

125. Think about the functions involved in your Service Lines project, what processes flow from these functions?
<--- Score

126. How can risk management be tied procedurally to process elements?
<--- Score

127. What qualifies as competition?

<--- Score

128. What is the cost of poor quality as supported by the team's analysis?
<--- Score

129. Do several people in different organizational units assist with the Service Lines process?
<--- Score

130. Do your employees have the opportunity to do what they do best everyday?
<--- Score

131. How will the change process be managed?
<--- Score

132. Where is the data coming from to measure compliance?
<--- Score

133. What tools were used to narrow the list of possible causes?
<--- Score

134. Think about some of the processes you undertake within your organization, which do you own?
<--- Score

Add up total points for this section:
_ _ _ _ _ = Total points for this section

Divided by: _ _ _ _ _ _ (number of statements answered) = _ _ _ _ _ _
Average score for this section

Transfer your score to the Service Lines
Index at the beginning of the Self-
Assessment.

CRITERION #5: IMPROVE:

INTENT: Develop a practical solution. Innovate, establish and test the solution and to measure the results.

In my belief, the answer to this question is clearly defined:

5 Strongly Agree

4 Agree

3 Neutral

2 Disagree

1 Strongly Disagree

1. Why improve in the first place?
<--- Score

2. How will you know that a change is an improvement?
<--- Score

3. How are Service Lines risks managed?
<--- Score

4. Is the solution technically practical?
<--- Score

5. Do you cover the five essential competencies: Communication, Collaboration, Innovation, Adaptability, and Leadership that improve an organizations ability to leverage the new Service Lines in a volatile global economy?
<--- Score

6. Is the measure of success for Service Lines understandable to a variety of people?
<--- Score

7. Are decisions made in a timely manner?
<--- Score

8. What are your current levels and trends in key measures or indicators of workforce and leader development?
<--- Score

9. Is any Service Lines documentation required?
<--- Score

10. Where do you need Service Lines improvement?
<--- Score

11. How do you measure risk?
<--- Score

12. How do you measure improved Service Lines service perception, and satisfaction?
<--- Score

13. What resources are required for the improvement efforts?
<--- Score

14. What were the underlying assumptions on the cost-benefit analysis?
<--- Score

15. What is the magnitude of the improvements?
<--- Score

16. Is the scope clearly documented?
<--- Score

17. How do you link measurement and risk?
<--- Score

18. Do you combine technical expertise with business knowledge and Service Lines Key topics include lifecycles, development approaches, requirements and how to make a business case?
<--- Score

19. How do you go about comparing Service Lines approaches/solutions?
<--- Score

20. When you map the key players in your own work and the types/domains of relationships with them, which relationships do you find easy and which challenging, and why?
<--- Score

21. Are the risks fully understood, reasonable and manageable?
<--- Score

22. How do you improve your likelihood of success ?
<--- Score

23. Who are the key stakeholders for the Service Lines evaluation?
<--- Score

24. What do you want to improve?
<--- Score

25. Was a Service Lines charter developed?
<--- Score

26. What does the 'should be' process map/design look like?
<--- Score

27. What are the affordable Service Lines risks?
<--- Score

28. What communications are necessary to support the implementation of the solution?
<--- Score

29. Who are the Service Lines decision-makers?
<--- Score

30. What tools were most useful during the improve phase?
<--- Score

31. What lessons, if any, from a pilot were incorporated into the design of the full-scale solution?
<--- Score

32. Do vendor agreements bring new compliance risk
?
<--- Score

33. Is supporting Service Lines documentation
required?
<--- Score

34. Are events managed to resolution?
<--- Score

35. What current systems have to be understood and/
or changed?
<--- Score

36. Can the solution be designed and implemented
within an acceptable time period?
<--- Score

37. How do you measure progress and evaluate
training effectiveness?
<--- Score

38. Service Lines risk decisions: whose call Is It?
<--- Score

39. How are policy decisions made and where?
<--- Score

40. What is Service Lines's impact on utilizing the best
solution(s)?
<--- Score

41. Who will be responsible for making the decisions
to include or exclude requested changes once Service
Lines is underway?

<--- Score

42. How significant is the improvement in the eyes of the end user?
<--- Score

43. How scalable is your Service Lines solution?
<--- Score

44. Does a good decision guarantee a good outcome?
<--- Score

45. Is the Service Lines risk managed?
<--- Score

46. How do you improve productivity?
<--- Score

47. Are procedures documented for managing Service Lines risks?
<--- Score

48. What assumptions are made about the solution and approach?
<--- Score

49. If you could go back in time five years, what decision would you make differently? What is your best guess as to what decision you're making today you might regret five years from now?
<--- Score

50. What practices helps your organization to develop its capacity to recognize patterns?
<--- Score

51. Who manages Service Lines risk?
<--- Score

52. What tools were used to evaluate the potential solutions?
<--- Score

53. How will you measure the results?
<--- Score

54. In the past few months, what is the smallest change you have made that has had the biggest positive result? What was it about that small change that produced the large return?
<--- Score

55. How will you know when its improved?
<--- Score

56. How do you decide how much to remunerate an employee?
<--- Score

57. How can you improve performance?
<--- Score

58. What criteria will you use to assess your Service Lines risks?
<--- Score

59. Explorations of the frontiers of Service Lines will help you build influence, improve Service Lines, optimize decision making, and sustain change, what is your approach?
<--- Score

60. What area needs the greatest improvement?
<--- Score

61. Is risk periodically assessed?
<--- Score

62. At what point will vulnerability assessments be performed once Service Lines is put into production (e.g., ongoing Risk Management after implementation)?
<--- Score

63. Is there a high likelihood that any recommendations will achieve their intended results?
<--- Score

64. Is Service Lines documentation maintained?
<--- Score

65. How risky is your organization?
<--- Score

66. Risk factors: what are the characteristics of Service Lines that make it risky?
<--- Score

67. What are the concrete Service Lines results?
<--- Score

68. Are risk triggers captured?
<--- Score

69. How do you deal with Service Lines risk?
<--- Score

70. For decision problems, how do you develop a

decision statement?
<--- Score

71. How can you improve Service Lines?
<--- Score

72. Is there any other Service Lines solution?
<--- Score

73. How do you engage, organize your business, develop your service lines?
<--- Score

74. Who makes the Service Lines decisions in your organization?
<--- Score

75. What went well, what should change, what can improve?
<--- Score

76. Does the goal represent a desired result that can be measured?
<--- Score

77. Who will be using the results of the measurement activities?
<--- Score

78. How is continuous improvement applied to risk management?
<--- Score

79. Who controls key decisions that will be made?
<--- Score

80. Have you achieved Service Lines improvements?
<--- Score

81. How will you recognize and celebrate results?
<--- Score

82. Do those selected for the Service Lines team have a good general understanding of what Service Lines is all about?
<--- Score

83. Is the Service Lines documentation thorough?
<--- Score

84. How do you manage and improve your Service Lines work systems to deliver customer value and achieve organizational success and sustainability?
<--- Score

85. How do you improve Service Lines service perception, and satisfaction?
<--- Score

86. Do you have the optimal project management team structure?
<--- Score

87. For estimation problems, how do you develop an estimation statement?
<--- Score

88. Who do you report Service Lines results to?
<--- Score

89. Which Service Lines solution is appropriate?
<--- Score

90. What is the team's contingency plan for potential problems occurring in implementation?
<--- Score

91. What are the expected Service Lines results?
<--- Score

92. How do you mitigate Service Lines risk?
<--- Score

93. What improvements have been achieved?
<--- Score

94. What can you do to improve?
<--- Score

95. Can you integrate quality management and risk management?
<--- Score

96. Where do the Service Lines decisions reside?
<--- Score

97. Who manages supplier risk management in your organization?
<--- Score

98. What alternative responses are available to manage risk?
<--- Score

99. What risks do you need to manage?
<--- Score

100. How can you better manage risk?

<--- Score

101. What should a proof of concept or pilot accomplish?
<--- Score

102. What strategies for Service Lines improvement are successful?
<--- Score

103. Risk events: what are the things that could go wrong?
<--- Score

104. What is the risk?
<--- Score

105. How does the team improve its work?
<--- Score

106. Are risk management tasks balanced centrally and locally?
<--- Score

107. How can skill-level changes improve Service Lines?
<--- Score

108. What were the criteria for evaluating a Service Lines pilot?
<--- Score

109. Who controls the risk?
<--- Score

110. Who are the people involved in developing and

implementing Service Lines?
<--- Score

111. Do you need to do a usability evaluation?
<--- Score

112. What is the Service Lines's sustainability risk?
<--- Score

113. How do you keep improving Service Lines?
<--- Score

114. What needs improvement? Why?
<--- Score

115. What Service Lines improvements can be made?
<--- Score

116. Have you identified breakpoints and/or risk tolerances that will trigger broad consideration of a potential need for intervention or modification of strategy?
<--- Score

117. Risk Identification: What are the possible risk events your organization faces in relation to Service Lines?
<--- Score

118. What tools do you use once you have decided on a Service Lines strategy and more importantly how do you choose?
<--- Score

119. Is the Service Lines solution sustainable?
<--- Score

120. Can you identify any significant risks or exposures to Service Lines third- parties (vendors, service providers, alliance partners etc) that concern you?
<--- Score

121. What is Service Lines risk?
<--- Score

122. What error proofing will be done to address some of the discrepancies observed in the 'as is' process?
<--- Score

123. Are the most efficient solutions problem-specific?
<--- Score

124. How is knowledge sharing about risk management improved?
<--- Score

125. Are the key business and technology risks being managed?
<--- Score

126. What are the Service Lines security risks?
<--- Score

127. To what extent does management recognize Service Lines as a tool to increase the results?
<--- Score

128. Who should make the Service Lines decisions?
<--- Score

129. How will you know that you have improved?
<--- Score

130. What is the implementation plan?
<--- Score

131. Who are the Service Lines decision makers?
<--- Score

132. How do you define the solutions' scope?
<--- Score

133. What tools were used to tap into the creativity and encourage 'outside the box' thinking?
<--- Score

134. Will the controls trigger any other risks?
<--- Score

135. How do the Service Lines results compare with the performance of your competitors and other organizations with similar offerings?
<--- Score

136. What are the implications of the one critical Service Lines decision 10 minutes, 10 months, and 10 years from now?
<--- Score

Add up total points for this section:
_ _ _ _ _ = Total points for this section

Divided by: _ _ _ _ _ _ (number of statements answered) = _ _ _ _ _ _
Average score for this section

Transfer your score to the Service Lines Index at the beginning of the Self-

Assessment.

CRITERION #6: CONTROL:

INTENT: Implement the practical solution. Maintain the performance and correct possible complications.

In my belief, the answer to this question is clearly defined:

5 Strongly Agree

4 Agree

3 Neutral

2 Disagree

1 Strongly Disagree

1. How will the process owner verify improvement in present and future sigma levels, process capabilities?
<--- Score

2. Is knowledge gained on process shared and institutionalized?
<--- Score

3. What is the recommended frequency of auditing?

<--- Score

4. Does job training on the documented procedures need to be part of the process team's education and training?
<--- Score

5. Is reporting being used or needed?
<--- Score

6. Can you adapt and adjust to changing Service Lines situations?
<--- Score

7. Will your goals reflect your program budget?
<--- Score

8. How do you monitor usage and cost?
<--- Score

9. Who is going to spread your message?
<--- Score

10. How do you select, collect, align, and integrate Service Lines data and information for tracking daily operations and overall organizational performance, including progress relative to strategic objectives and action plans?
<--- Score

11. What key inputs and outputs are being measured on an ongoing basis?
<--- Score

12. In the case of a Service Lines project, the criteria for the audit derive from implementation objectives,

an audit of a Service Lines project involves assessing whether the recommendations outlined for implementation have been met, can you track that any Service Lines project is implemented as planned, and is it working?
<--- Score

13. Will any special training be provided for results interpretation?
<--- Score

14. Who will be in control?
<--- Score

15. What other areas of the group might benefit from the Service Lines team's improvements, knowledge, and learning?
<--- Score

16. What is your theory of human motivation, and how does your compensation plan fit with that view?
<--- Score

17. What are the performance and scale of the Service Lines tools?
<--- Score

18. What are the known security controls?
<--- Score

19. What are the key elements of your Service Lines performance improvement system, including your evaluation, organizational learning, and innovation processes?
<--- Score

20. Has the improved process and its steps been standardized?
<--- Score

21. What quality tools were useful in the control phase?
<--- Score

22. Are new process steps, standards, and documentation ingrained into normal operations?
<--- Score

23. What should you measure to verify efficiency gains?
<--- Score

24. Is new knowledge gained imbedded in the response plan?
<--- Score

25. Do you monitor the Service Lines decisions made and fine tune them as they evolve?
<--- Score

26. What is the best design framework for Service Lines organization now that, in a post industrial-age if the top-down, command and control model is no longer relevant?
<--- Score

27. Do the Service Lines decisions you make today help people and the planet tomorrow?
<--- Score

28. Is there a documented and implemented monitoring plan?

<--- Score

29. Are documented procedures clear and easy to follow for the operators?
<--- Score

30. How is Service Lines project cost planned, managed, monitored?
<--- Score

31. What are your results for key measures or indicators of the accomplishment of your Service Lines strategy and action plans, including building and strengthening core competencies?
<--- Score

32. How will input, process, and output variables be checked to detect for sub-optimal conditions?
<--- Score

33. Who has control over resources?
<--- Score

34. You may have created your quality measures at a time when you lacked resources, technology wasn't up to the required standard, or low service levels were the industry norm. Have those circumstances changed?
<--- Score

35. Are there documented procedures?
<--- Score

36. What should the next improvement project be that is related to Service Lines?
<--- Score

37. Are you measuring, monitoring and predicting Service Lines activities to optimize operations and profitability, and enhancing outcomes?
<--- Score

38. Is there documentation that will support the successful operation of the improvement?
<--- Score

39. Are suggested corrective/restorative actions indicated on the response plan for known causes to problems that might surface?
<--- Score

40. Do you monitor the effectiveness of your Service Lines activities?
<--- Score

41. Is a response plan established and deployed?
<--- Score

42. What do you stand for--and what are you against?
<--- Score

43. Is there a transfer of ownership and knowledge to process owner and process team tasked with the responsibilities.
<--- Score

44. Where do ideas that reach policy makers and planners as proposals for Service Lines strengthening and reform actually originate?
<--- Score

45. How do you encourage people to take control and

responsibility?
<--- Score

46. What other systems, operations, processes, and infrastructures (hiring practices, staffing, training, incentives/rewards, metrics/dashboards/scorecards, etc.) need updates, additions, changes, or deletions in order to facilitate knowledge transfer and improvements?
<--- Score

47. Can support from partners be adjusted?
<--- Score

48. What do your reports reflect?
<--- Score

49. Act/Adjust: What Do you Need to Do Differently?
<--- Score

50. How will new or emerging customer needs/requirements be checked/communicated to orient the process toward meeting the new specifications and continually reducing variation?
<--- Score

51. What are the critical parameters to watch?
<--- Score

52. How can you best use all of your knowledge repositories to enhance learning and sharing?
<--- Score

53. What are you attempting to measure/monitor?
<--- Score

54. Does a troubleshooting guide exist or is it needed?
<--- Score

55. What adjustments to the strategies are needed?
<--- Score

56. Are pertinent alerts monitored, analyzed and distributed to appropriate personnel?
<--- Score

57. What is the standard for acceptable Service Lines performance?
<--- Score

58. Do the viable solutions scale to future needs?
<--- Score

59. Who controls critical resources?
<--- Score

60. Are the Service Lines standards challenging?
<--- Score

61. What can you control?
<--- Score

62. How do your controls stack up?
<--- Score

63. How do you establish and deploy modified action plans if circumstances require a shift in plans and rapid execution of new plans?
<--- Score

64. Is there an action plan in case of emergencies?
<--- Score

65. How is change control managed?
<--- Score

66. Is a response plan in place for when the input, process, or output measures indicate an 'out-of-control' condition?
<--- Score

67. Is there a control plan in place for sustaining improvements (short and long-term)?
<--- Score

68. Is there a standardized process?
<--- Score

69. Does the response plan contain a definite closed loop continual improvement scheme (e.g., plan-do-check-act)?
<--- Score

70. Does the Service Lines performance meet the customer's requirements?
<--- Score

71. How do you spread information?
<--- Score

72. Have new or revised work instructions resulted?
<--- Score

73. How do you plan for the cost of succession?
<--- Score

74. How will the process owner and team be able to hold the gains?

<--- Score

75. What do you measure to verify effectiveness gains?
<--- Score

76. What Service Lines standards are applicable?
<--- Score

77. How might the group capture best practices and lessons learned so as to leverage improvements?
<--- Score

78. How will you measure your QA plan's effectiveness?
<--- Score

79. Is there a Service Lines Communication plan covering who needs to get what information when?
<--- Score

80. Implementation Planning: is a pilot needed to test the changes before a full roll out occurs?
<--- Score

81. Is there a recommended audit plan for routine surveillance inspections of Service Lines's gains?
<--- Score

82. Are the planned controls in place?
<--- Score

83. Has the Service Lines value of standards been quantified?
<--- Score

84. Will the team be available to assist members in planning investigations?
<--- Score

85. Who sets the Service Lines standards?
<--- Score

86. What are customers monitoring?
<--- Score

87. What is your plan to assess your security risks?
<--- Score

88. How do you plan on providing proper recognition and disclosure of supporting companies?
<--- Score

89. Are controls in place and consistently applied?
<--- Score

90. How do senior leaders actions reflect a commitment to the organizations Service Lines values?
<--- Score

91. How will report readings be checked to effectively monitor performance?
<--- Score

92. Does Service Lines appropriately measure and monitor risk?
<--- Score

93. How likely is the current Service Lines plan to come in on schedule or on budget?
<--- Score

94. How do controls support value?
<--- Score

95. Who is the Service Lines process owner?
<--- Score

96. How will the day-to-day responsibilities for monitoring and continual improvement be transferred from the improvement team to the process owner?
<--- Score

97. How widespread is its use?
<--- Score

98. What is the control/monitoring plan?
<--- Score

99. How will Service Lines decisions be made and monitored?
<--- Score

100. Are operating procedures consistent?
<--- Score

Add up total points for this section:
_____ = Total points for this section

Divided by: _____ (number of statements answered) = _____
Average score for this section

Transfer your score to the Service Lines Index at the beginning of the Self-Assessment.

CRITERION #7: SUSTAIN:

INTENT: Retain the benefits.

In my belief, the answer to this
question is clearly defined:

5 Strongly Agree

4 Agree

3 Neutral

2 Disagree

1 Strongly Disagree

1. Are you maintaining a past–present–future
perspective throughout the Service Lines discussion?
<--- Score

2. If no one would ever find out about your
accomplishments, how would you lead differently?
<--- Score

3. How do you determine the key elements that affect
Service Lines workforce satisfaction, how are these
elements determined for different workforce groups

and segments?
<--- Score

4. What will be the consequences to the stakeholder (financial, reputation etc) if Service Lines does not go ahead or fails to deliver the objectives?
<--- Score

5. Do you feel that more should be done in the Service Lines area?
<--- Score

6. Did your employees make progress today?
<--- Score

7. What would you recommend your friend do if he/she were facing this dilemma?
<--- Score

8. How important is Service Lines to the user organizations mission?
<--- Score

9. How do you provide a safe environment -physically and emotionally?
<--- Score

10. What should you stop doing?
<--- Score

11. What are strategies for increasing support and reducing opposition?
<--- Score

12. What are current Service Lines paradigms?
<--- Score

13. Is Service Lines dependent on the successful delivery of a current project?
<--- Score

14. How do you transition from the baseline to the target?
<--- Score

15. Is your basic point _____ or _____?
<--- Score

16. Is there any reason to believe the opposite of my current belief?
<--- Score

17. Who will provide the final approval of Service Lines deliverables?
<--- Score

18. Who, on the executive team or the board, has spoken to a customer recently?
<--- Score

19. What is the kind of project structure that would be appropriate for your Service Lines project, should it be formal and complex, or can it be less formal and relatively simple?
<--- Score

20. How do you make it meaningful in connecting Service Lines with what users do day-to-day?
<--- Score

21. How do you stay inspired?
<--- Score

22. Are you paying enough attention to the partners your company depends on to succeed?
<--- Score

23. How are you doing compared to your industry?
<--- Score

24. If you weren't already in this business, would you enter it today? And if not, what are you going to do about it?
<--- Score

25. Are the assumptions believable and achievable?
<--- Score

26. Why should people listen to you?
<--- Score

27. Is a Service Lines team work effort in place?
<--- Score

28. What may be the consequences for the performance of an organization if all stakeholders are not consulted regarding Service Lines?
<--- Score

29. What are your personal philosophies regarding Service Lines and how do they influence your work?
<--- Score

30. Do you see more potential in people than they do in themselves?
<--- Score

31. What is the big Service Lines idea?

<--- Score

32. At what moment would you think; Will I get fired?
<--- Score

33. Can you break it down?
<--- Score

34. Which Service Lines goals are the most important?
<--- Score

35. Why is it important to have senior management support for a Service Lines project?
<--- Score

36. Who else should you help?
<--- Score

37. How do you cross-sell and up-sell your Service Lines success?
<--- Score

38. What new services of functionality will be implemented next with Service Lines ?
<--- Score

39. How can you negotiate Service Lines successfully with a stubborn boss, an irate client, or a deceitful coworker?
<--- Score

40. Instead of going to current contacts for new ideas, what if you reconnected with dormant contacts--
the people you used to know? If you were going reactivate a dormant tie, who would it be?
<--- Score

41. How do you assess the Service Lines pitfalls that are inherent in implementing it?
<--- Score

42. What was the last experiment you ran?
<--- Score

43. If you do not follow, then how to lead?
<--- Score

44. What knowledge, skills and characteristics mark a good Service Lines project manager?
<--- Score

45. Do you have the right capabilities and capacities?
<--- Score

46. Do you think you know, or do you know you know ?
<--- Score

47. Do you know who is a friend or a foe?
<--- Score

48. How do you engage the workforce, in addition to satisfying them?
<--- Score

49. Who uses your product in ways you never expected?
<--- Score

50. How can you become the company that would put you out of business?
<--- Score

51. Can the schedule be done in the given time?
<--- Score

52. What is the range of capabilities?
<--- Score

53. Is there a work around that you can use?
<--- Score

54. If there were zero limitations, what would you do differently?
<--- Score

55. Who will manage the integration of tools?
<--- Score

56. What is the overall talent health of your organization as a whole at senior levels, and for each organization reporting to a member of the Senior Leadership Team?
<--- Score

57. If you had to rebuild your organization without any traditional competitive advantages (i.e., no killer technology, promising research, innovative product/ service delivery model, etcetera), how would your people have to approach their work and collaborate together in order to create the necessary conditions for success?
<--- Score

58. How do you accomplish your long range Service Lines goals?
<--- Score

59. Are assumptions made in Service Lines stated explicitly?
<--- Score

60. What are the key enablers to make this Service Lines move?
<--- Score

61. What is an unauthorized commitment?
<--- Score

62. Are you changing as fast as the world around you?
<--- Score

63. How do you track customer value, profitability or financial return, organizational success, and sustainability?
<--- Score

64. What are the success criteria that will indicate that Service Lines objectives have been met and the benefits delivered?
<--- Score

65. Are you making progress, and are you making progress as Service Lines leaders?
<--- Score

66. In the past year, what have you done (or could you have done) to increase the accurate perception of your company/brand as ethical and honest?
<--- Score

67. How do you keep records, of what?
<--- Score

68. Who do we want your customers to become?
<--- Score

69. What are the business goals Service Lines is aiming to achieve?
<--- Score

70. What is the purpose of Service Lines in relation to the mission?
<--- Score

71. Who is the main stakeholder, with ultimate responsibility for driving Service Lines forward?
<--- Score

72. What role does communication play in the success or failure of a Service Lines project?
<--- Score

73. How do you proactively clarify deliverables and Service Lines quality expectations?
<--- Score

74. How do you keep the momentum going?
<--- Score

75. What are the challenges?
<--- Score

76. Which models, tools and techniques are necessary?
<--- Score

77. What projects are going on in the organization today, and what resources are those projects using from the resource pools?

<--- Score

78. Who are your customers?
<--- Score

79. What is your competitive advantage?
<--- Score

80. Do you know what you are doing? And who do you call if you don't?
<--- Score

81. Do you have the right people on the bus?
<--- Score

82. Which functions and people interact with the supplier and or customer?
<--- Score

83. What management system can you use to leverage the Service Lines experience, ideas, and concerns of the people closest to the work to be done?
<--- Score

84. How do you know if you are successful?
<--- Score

85. What must you excel at?
<--- Score

86. How do you manage Service Lines Knowledge Management (KM)?
<--- Score

87. What is the craziest thing you can do?

<--- Score

88. How is implementation research currently incorporated into each of your goals?
<--- Score

89. How do you go about securing Service Lines?
<--- Score

90. What is your Service Lines strategy?
<--- Score

91. Will there be any necessary staff changes (redundancies or new hires)?
<--- Score

92. Are you using a design thinking approach and integrating Innovation, Service Lines Experience, and Brand Value?
<--- Score

93. Are the criteria for selecting recommendations stated?
<--- Score

94. Are you / should you be revolutionary or evolutionary?
<--- Score

95. What is your formula for success in Service Lines ?
<--- Score

96. What business benefits will Service Lines goals deliver if achieved?
<--- Score

97. Are you relevant? Will you be relevant five years from now? Ten?
<--- Score

98. What information is critical to your organization that your executives are ignoring?
<--- Score

99. How do you ensure that implementations of Service Lines products are done in a way that ensures safety?
<--- Score

100. How do senior leaders deploy your organizations vision and values through your leadership system, to the workforce, to key suppliers and partners, and to customers and other stakeholders, as appropriate?
<--- Score

101. Who is responsible for errors?
<--- Score

102. How do you maintain Service Lines's Integrity?
<--- Score

103. How will you know that the Service Lines project has been successful?
<--- Score

104. What types of service lines are missing?
<--- Score

105. Who are the key stakeholders?
<--- Score

106. What is effective Service Lines?

<--- Score

107. How long will it take to change?
<--- Score

108. In retrospect, of the projects that you pulled the plug on, what percent do you wish had been allowed to keep going, and what percent do you wish had ended earlier?
<--- Score

109. Who are four people whose careers you have enhanced?
<--- Score

110. What is something you believe that nearly no one agrees with you on?
<--- Score

111. Ask yourself: how would you do this work if you only had one staff member to do it?
<--- Score

112. How much contingency will be available in the budget?
<--- Score

113. Do you say no to customers for no reason?
<--- Score

114. If your customer were your grandmother, would you tell her to buy what you're selling?
<--- Score

115. What are you challenging?
<--- Score

116. Do you have enough freaky customers in your portfolio pushing you to the limit day in and day out?
<--- Score

117. Has implementation been effective in reaching specified objectives so far?
<--- Score

118. Do Service Lines rules make a reasonable demand on a users capabilities?
<--- Score

119. How do you listen to customers to obtain actionable information?
<--- Score

120. What are the usability implications of Service Lines actions?
<--- Score

121. What Service Lines skills are most important?
<--- Score

122. To whom do you add value?
<--- Score

123. If you had to leave your organization for a year and the only communication you could have with employees/colleagues was a single paragraph, what would you write?
<--- Score

124. What stupid rule would you most like to kill?
<--- Score

125. Why not do Service Lines?
<--- Score

126. When information truly is ubiquitous, when reach and connectivity are completely global, when computing resources are infinite, and when a whole new set of impossibilities are not only possible, but happening, what will that do to your business?
<--- Score

127. If you find that you havent accomplished one of the goals for one of the steps of the Service Lines strategy, what will you do to fix it?
<--- Score

128. Why will customers want to buy your organizations products/services?
<--- Score

129. Is the Service Lines organization completing tasks effectively and efficiently?
<--- Score

130. Marketing budgets are tighter, consumers are more skeptical, and social media has changed forever the way we talk about Service Lines, how do you gain traction?
<--- Score

131. What are your most important goals for the strategic Service Lines objectives?
<--- Score

132. If your company went out of business tomorrow, would anyone who doesn't get a paycheck here care?
<--- Score

133. What happens if you do not have enough funding?
<--- Score

134. What happens at your organization when people fail?
<--- Score

135. Political -is anyone trying to undermine this project?
<--- Score

136. Are all key stakeholders present at all Structured Walkthroughs?
<--- Score

137. Do you think Service Lines accomplishes the goals you expect it to accomplish?
<--- Score

138. What are internal and external Service Lines relations?
<--- Score

139. Whom among your colleagues do you trust, and for what?
<--- Score

140. Who do you want your customers to become?
<--- Score

141. What is your BATNA (best alternative to a negotiated agreement)?
<--- Score

142. What is your area of operation - by service lines?
<--- Score

143. Do you have an implicit bias for capital investments over people investments?
<--- Score

144. Is there any existing Service Lines governance structure?
<--- Score

145. How do you deal with Service Lines changes?
<--- Score

146. Who will be responsible for deciding whether Service Lines goes ahead or not after the initial investigations?
<--- Score

147. What is your question? Why?
<--- Score

148. Would you rather sell to knowledgeable and informed customers or to uninformed customers?
<--- Score

149. What threat is Service Lines addressing?
<--- Score

150. What one word do you want to own in the minds of your customers, employees, and partners?
<--- Score

151. How will you ensure you get what you expected?
<--- Score

152. Operational - will it work?
<--- Score

153. Who will determine interim and final deadlines?
<--- Score

154. What are the top 3 things at the forefront of your Service Lines agendas for the next 3 years?
<--- Score

155. What Service Lines modifications can you make work for you?
<--- Score

156. Why do and why don't your customers like your organization?
<--- Score

157. Are you satisfied with your current role? If not, what is missing from it?
<--- Score

158. In a project to restructure Service Lines outcomes, which stakeholders would you involve?
<--- Score

159. What potential megatrends could make your business model obsolete?
<--- Score

160. What are the short and long-term Service Lines goals?
<--- Score

161. What you are going to do to affect the numbers?

<--- Score

162. Will it be accepted by users?
<--- Score

163. What would have to be true for the option on the table to be the best possible choice?
<--- Score

164. How likely is it that a customer would recommend your company to a friend or colleague?
<--- Score

165. How do you govern and fulfill your societal responsibilities?
<--- Score

166. What is it like to work for you?
<--- Score

167. How can you incorporate support to ensure safe and effective use of Service Lines into the services that you provide?
<--- Score

168. What are you trying to prove to yourself, and how might it be hijacking your life and business success?
<--- Score

169. What happens when a new employee joins the organization?
<--- Score

170. What are specific Service Lines rules to follow?
<--- Score

171. Where can you break convention?
<--- Score

172. What counts that you are not counting?
<--- Score

173. Why is Service Lines important for you now?
<--- Score

174. What have been your experiences in defining long range Service Lines goals?
<--- Score

175. Is maximizing Service Lines protection the same as minimizing Service Lines loss?
<--- Score

176. What is the recommended frequency of auditing?
<--- Score

177. How much does Service Lines help?
<--- Score

178. Is a Service Lines breakthrough on the horizon?
<--- Score

179. Why should you adopt a Service Lines framework?
<--- Score

180. Can you maintain your growth without detracting from the factors that have contributed to your success?
<--- Score

181. What could happen if you do not do it?

<--- Score

182. What is the overall business strategy?
<--- Score

183. Think of your Service Lines project, what are the main functions?
<--- Score

184. Who is responsible for ensuring appropriate resources (time, people and money) are allocated to Service Lines?
<--- Score

185. What is the estimated value of the project?
<--- Score

186. How do you set Service Lines stretch targets and how do you get people to not only participate in setting these stretch targets but also that they strive to achieve these?
<--- Score

187. Is Service Lines realistic, or are you setting yourself up for failure?
<--- Score

188. How will you insure seamless interoperability of Service Lines moving forward?
<--- Score

189. Who is responsible for Service Lines?
<--- Score

190. What are the potential basics of Service Lines fraud?

<--- Score

191. What is the source of the strategies for Service Lines strengthening and reform?
<--- Score

192. How do you foster the skills, knowledge, talents, attributes, and characteristics you want to have?
<--- Score

193. Who have you, as a company, historically been when you've been at your best?
<--- Score

194. Are there any activities that you can take off your to do list?
<--- Score

195. How will you motivate the stakeholders with the least vested interest?
<--- Score

196. If you were responsible for initiating and implementing major changes in your organization, what steps might you take to ensure acceptance of those changes?
<--- Score

197. What are the barriers to increased Service Lines production?
<--- Score

198. What unique value proposition (UVP) do you offer?
<--- Score

199. Do you have past Service Lines successes?
<--- Score

200. What relationships among Service Lines trends do you perceive?
<--- Score

201. What are the rules and assumptions your industry operates under? What if the opposite were true?
<--- Score

202. If you got fired and a new hire took your place, what would she do different?
<--- Score

203. What trouble can you get into?
<--- Score

204. Are your responses positive or negative?
<--- Score

205. How can you become more high-tech but still be high touch?
<--- Score

206. What trophy do you want on your mantle?
<--- Score

207. What does your signature ensure?
<--- Score

Add up total points for this section:
_ _ _ _ _ = Total points for this section

Divided by: _ _ _ _ _ _ (number of statements answered) = _ _ _ _ _ _

Average score for this section

Transfer your score to the Service Lines
Index at the beginning of the Self-
Assessment.

Service Lines and Managing Projects, Criteria for Project Managers:

1.0 Initiating Process Group: Service Lines

1. Who supports, improves, and oversees standardized processes related to the Service Lines projects program?

2. Does it make any difference if you am successful?

3. How do you help others satisfy needs?

4. How to control and approve each phase?

5. When must it be done?

6. How will it affect me?

7. Were resources available as planned?

8. Mitigate. what will you do to minimize the impact should the risk event occur?

9. How should needs be met?

10. Specific - is the objective clear in terms of what, how, when, and where the situation will be changed?

11. How will you know you did it?

12. For technology Service Lines projects only:
Are all production support stakeholders (Business unit, technical support, & user) prepared for implementation with appropriate contingency plans?

13. What are the short and long term implications?

14. What were things that you did well, and could improve, and how?

15. Have the stakeholders identified all individual requirements pertaining to business process?

16. First of all, should any action be taken?

17. Did the Service Lines project team have the right skills?

18. Where must it be done?

19. What technical work to do in each phase?

20. If the risk event occurs, what will you do?

1.1 Project Charter: Service Lines

21. What are you striving to accomplish (measurable goal(s))?

22. Who will take notes, document decisions?

23. Did your Service Lines project ask for this?

24. Who manages integration?

25. Are you building in-house ?

26. Why use a Service Lines project charter?

27. What changes can you make to improve?

28. Major high-level milestone targets: what events measure progress?

29. Why have you chosen the aim you have set forth?

30. Who are the stakeholders?

31. Assumptions: what factors, for planning purposes, are you considering to be true?

32. Environmental stewardship and sustainability considerations: what is the process that will be used to ensure compliance with the environmental stewardship policy?

33. Service Lines project objective statement: what must the Service Lines project do?

34. Assumptions and constraints: what assumptions were made in defining the Service Lines project?

35. If finished, on what date did it finish?

36. Service Lines project background: what is the primary motivation for this Service Lines project?

37. Does the Service Lines project need to consider any special capacity or capability issues?

38. How will you know that a change is an improvement?

39. Why do you manage integration?

40. When will this occur?

1.2 Stakeholder Register: Service Lines

41. What are the major Service Lines project milestones requiring communications or providing communications opportunities?

42. Who wants to talk about Security?

43. Who is managing stakeholder engagement?

44. What & Why?

45. Is your organization ready for change?

46. What is the power of the stakeholder?

47. What opportunities exist to provide communications?

48. How much influence do they have on the Service Lines project?

49. How should employers make voices heard?

50. How will reports be created?

51. How big is the gap?

1.3 Stakeholder Analysis Matrix: Service Lines

52. Who is most dependent on the resources at stake?

53. Identify the stakeholders levels most frequently used –or at least sought– in your Service Lines projects and for which purpose?

54. How to measure the achievement of the Immediate Objective?

55. What do you Evaluate?

56. Processes, systems, it, communications?

57. Effects on core activities, distraction?

58. Global influences?

59. Alliances: with which other actors is the actor allied, how are they interconnected?

60. Who has control over whom?

61. Cultural, attitudinal, behavioural?

62. Who is influential in the Service Lines project area (both thematic and geographic areas)?

63. Are the required specifications for products or services changing?

64. Are the interests in line with the program objectives?

65. Sustainable financial backing?

66. Who are potential allies and opponents?

67. Lack of competitive strength?

68. What is the issue at stake?

69. Gaps in capabilities?

70. Are they likely to influence the success or failure of your Service Lines project?

71. Who determines value?

2.0 Planning Process Group: Service Lines

72. On which process should team members spend the most time?

73. Explanation: is what the Service Lines project intents to solve a hard question?

74. How will it affect you?

75. Why do it Service Lines projects fail?

76. To what extent has the intervention strategy been adapted to the areas of intervention in which it is being implemented?

77. What input will you be required to provide the Service Lines project team?

78. If you are late, will anybody notice?

79. To what extent is the program helping to influence your organizations policy framework?

80. What should you do next?

81. To what extent do the intervention objectives and strategies of the Service Lines project respond to your organizations plans?

82. What is the critical path for this Service Lines project, and what is the duration of the critical path?

83. How many days can task X be late in starting without affecting the Service Lines project completion date?

84. To what extent are the visions and actions of the partners consistent or divergent with regard to the program?

85. If action is called for, what form should it take?

86. Why is it important to determine activity sequencing on Service Lines projects?

87. Are there efficient coordination mechanisms to avoid overloading the counterparts, participating stakeholders?

88. How well did the chosen processes fit the needs of the Service Lines project?

89. What is the NEXT thing to do?

90. Are the necessary foundations in place to ensure the sustainability of the results of the Service Lines project?

2.1 Project Management Plan: Service Lines

91. Will you add a schedule and diagram?

92. Is mitigation authorized or recommended?

93. Who is the sponsor?

94. What went right?

95. How do you organize the costs in the Service Lines project management plan?

96. Do the proposed changes from the Service Lines project include any significant risks to safety?

97. Development trends and opportunities. What if the positive direction and vision of your organization causes expected trends to change?

98. What worked well?

99. What is Service Lines project scope management?

100. Does the implementation plan have an appropriate division of responsibilities?

101. Is the engineering content at a feasibility level-of-detail, and is it sufficiently complete, to provide an adequate basis for the baseline cost estimate?

102. Who is the Service Lines project Manager?

103. Has the selected plan been formulated using cost effectiveness and incremental analysis techniques?

104. Are there any windfall benefits that would accrue to the Service Lines project sponsor or other parties?

105. If the Service Lines project is complex or scope is specialized, do you have appropriate and/or qualified staff available to perform the tasks?

106. What are the constraints?

107. What would you do differently what did not work?

108. Are calculations and results of analyzes essentially correct?

109. Is there anything you would now do differently on your Service Lines project based on past experience?

2.2 Scope Management Plan: Service Lines

110. Has a capability assessment been conducted?

111. Are there any windfall benefits that would accrue to the Service Lines project sponsor or other parties?

112. What does the critical path really mean?

113. Are actuals compared against estimates to analyze and correct variances?

114. Has the scope management document been updated and distributed to help prevent scope creep?

115. Are any non-compliance issues that exist due to organizations practices?

116. Has a quality assurance plan been developed for the Service Lines project?

117. Was the scope definition used in task sequencing?

118. Is an industry recognized mechanized support tool(s) being used for Service Lines project scheduling & tracking?

119. Are tasks tracked by hours?

120. Are post milestone Service Lines project reviews (PMPR) conducted with your organization at least

once a year?

121. Is each item clearly and completely defined?

122. Who is responsible for monitoring the Service Lines project scope to ensure the Service Lines project remains within the scope baseline?

123. Are Service Lines project team members committed fulltime?

124. Deliverables -are the deliverables tangible and verifiable?

125. What if you do not have more detailed information on the report?

126. Why do you need to manage scope?

127. Have key stakeholders been identified?

128. Is there an on-going process in place to monitor Service Lines project risks?

129. What are the risks that could significantly affect the budget of the Service Lines project?

2.3 Requirements Management Plan: Service Lines

130. Is any organizational data being used or stored?

131. Who will perform the analysis?

132. Describe the process for rejecting the Service Lines project requirements. Who has the authority to reject Service Lines project requirements?

133. Do you have an appropriate arrangement for meetings?

134. When and how will a requirements baseline be established in this Service Lines project?

135. How often will the reporting occur?

136. Will the contractors involved take full responsibility?

137. How will the requirements become prioritized?

138. Did you use declarative statements?

139. What cost metrics will be used?

140. Did you distinguish the scope of work the contractor(s) will be required to do?

141. Is it new or replacing an existing business system or process?

142. The wbs is developed as part of a joint planning session. and how do you know that youhave done this right?

143. Subject to change control?

144. Do you really need to write this document at all?

145. Is requirements work dependent on any other specific Service Lines project or non-Service Lines project activities (e.g. funding, approvals, procurement)?

146. Have stakeholders been instructed in the Change Control process?

147. In case of software development; Should you have a test for each code module?

148. Is there formal agreement on who has authority to request a change in requirements?

2.4 Requirements Documentation: Service Lines

149. Can you check system requirements?

150. Are there any requirements conflicts?

151. How do you know when a Requirement is accurate enough?

152. What is the risk associated with the technology?

153. What images does it conjure?

154. Where do system and software requirements come from, what are sources?

155. What can tools do for us?

156. How will the proposed Service Lines project help?

157. The problem with gathering requirements is right there in the word gathering. What images does it conjure?

158. What is a show stopper in the requirements?

159. Where are business rules being captured?

160. What are current process problems?

161. Can the requirement be changed without a large

impact on other requirements?

162. How does the proposed Service Lines project contribute to the overall objectives of your organization?

163. Validity. does the system provide the functions which best support the customers needs?

164. What if the system wasn t implemented?

165. Do your constraints stand?

166. If applicable; are there issues linked with the fact that this is an offshore Service Lines project?

167. What happens when requirements are wrong?

168. How much testing do you need to do to prove that your system is safe?

2.5 Requirements Traceability Matrix: Service Lines

169. How will it affect the stakeholders personally in career?

170. How small is small enough?

171. What are the chronologies, contingencies, consequences, criteria?

172. Will you use a Requirements Traceability Matrix?

173. How do you manage scope?

174. Is there a requirements traceability process in place?

175. Why use a WBS?

176. Describe the process for approving requirements so they can be added to the traceability matrix and Service Lines project work can be performed. Will the Service Lines project requirements become approved in writing?

177. What is the WBS?

178. What percentage of Service Lines projects are producing traceability matrices between requirements and other work products?

179. Why do you manage scope?

180. Do you have a clear understanding of all subcontracts in place?

2.6 Project Scope Statement: Service Lines

181. Who will you recommend approve the change, and when do you recommend the change reviews occur?

182. If the scope changes, what will the impact be to your Service Lines project in terms of duration, cost, quality, or any other important areas of the Service Lines project?

183. Is this process communicated to the customer and team members?

184. Is the plan for your organization of the Service Lines project resources adequate?

185. Will the qa related information be reported regularly as part of the status reporting mechanisms?

186. Are there issues that could affect the existing requirements for the result, service, or product if the scope changes?

187. Elements that deal with providing the detail?

188. Is the Service Lines project sponsor function identified and defined?

189. Is the plan under configuration management?

190. Will there be a Change Control Process in place?

191. Has the format for tracking and monitoring schedules and costs been defined?

192. How will you verify the accuracy of the work of the Service Lines project, and what constitutes acceptance of the deliverables?

193. Do you anticipate new stakeholders joining the Service Lines project over time?

194. Is the Service Lines project organization documented and on file?

195. Have you been able to thoroughly document the Service Lines projects assumptions and constraints?

196. Were potential customers involved early in the planning process?

197. Which risks does the Service Lines project focus on?

198. What should you drop in order to add something new?

199. Is the scope of your Service Lines project well defined?

200. What is the most common tool for helping define the detail?

2.7 Assumption and Constraint Log: Service Lines

201. Does the document/deliverable meet all requirements (for example, statement of work) specific to this deliverable?

202. Are there processes defining how software will be developed including development methods, overall timeline for development, software product standards, and traceability?

203. Does the system design reflect the requirements?

204. How do you design an auditing system?

205. Contradictory information between different documents?

206. Would known impacts serve as impediments?

207. Can the requirements be traced to the appropriate components of the solution, as well as test scripts?

208. Violation trace: why ?

209. Is the definition of the Service Lines project scope clear; what needs to be accomplished?

210. Has a Service Lines project Communications Plan been developed?

211. If it is out of compliance, should the process be amended or should the Plan be amended?

212. Are there nonconformance issues?

213. What other teams / processes would be impacted by changes to the current process, and how?

214. Is the steering committee active in Service Lines project oversight?

215. Are there ways to reduce the time it takes to get something approved?

216. Is the process working, and people are not executing in compliance of the process?

217. Contradictory information between document sections?

218. Model-building: what data-analytic strategies are useful when building proportional-hazards models?

219. What weaknesses do you have?

220. How many Service Lines project staff does this specific process affect?

2.8 Work Breakdown Structure: Service Lines

221. How much detail?

222. Why is it useful?

223. Do you need another level?

224. How will you and your Service Lines project team define the Service Lines projects scope and work breakdown structure?

225. Is it a change in scope?

226. Is the work breakdown structure (wbs) defined and is the scope of the Service Lines project clear with assigned deliverable owners?

227. Who has to do it?

228. When does it have to be done?

229. What is the probability that the Service Lines project duration will exceed xx weeks?

230. What has to be done?

231. How far down?

232. When would you develop a Work Breakdown Structure?

233. When do you stop?

234. Why would you develop a Work Breakdown Structure?

235. How big is a work-package?

236. Where does it take place?

2.9 WBS Dictionary: Service Lines

237. Do the lines of authority for incurring indirect costs correspond to the lines of responsibility for management control of the same components of costs?

238. Are your organizations and items of cost assigned to each pool identified?

239. Are data elements summarized through the functional organizational structure for progressively higher levels of management?

240. Are data elements (BCWS, BCWP, and ACWP) progressively summarized from the detail level to the contract level through the CWBS?

241. Identify potential or actual overruns and underruns?

242. Are all authorized tasks assigned to identified organizational elements?

243. Where learning is used in developing underlying budgets is there a direct relationship between anticipated learning and time phased budgets?

244. Are work packages reasonably short in time duration or do they have adequate objective indicators/milestones to minimize subjectivity of the in process work evaluation?

245. Identify and isolate causes of favorable and

unfavorable cost and schedule variances?

246. Contemplated overhead expenditure for each period based on the best information currently available?

247. Are retroactive changes to budgets for completed work specifically prohibited in an established procedure, and is this procedure adhered to?

248. Is work progressively subdivided into detailed work packages as requirements are defined?

249. The total budget for the contract (including estimates for authorized and unpriced work)?

250. Are authorized changes being incorporated in a timely manner?

251. Does the contractors system description or procedures require that the performance measurement baseline plus management reserve equal the contract budget base?

252. Are retroactive changes to direct costs and indirect costs prohibited except for the correction of errors and routine accounting adjustments?

253. Does the contractors system provide unit costs, equivalent unit or lot costs in terms of labor, material, other direct, and indirect costs?

254. Is the work done on a work package level as described in the WBS dictionary?

255. Wbs elements contractually specified for reporting of status to you (lowest level only)?

256. Where engineering standards or other internal work measurement systems are used, is there a formal relationship between corresponding values and work package budgets?

2.10 Schedule Management Plan: Service Lines

257. Is a pmo (Service Lines project management office) in place and provide oversight to the Service Lines project?

258. Personnel with expertise?

259. Staffing Requirements?

260. Is the steering committee active in Service Lines project oversight?

261. Has a sponsor been identified?

262. Does all Service Lines project documentation reside in a common repository for easy access?

263. Are Service Lines project team members involved in detailed estimating and scheduling?

264. What date will the task finish?

265. Are decisions captured in a decisions log?

266. Is funded schedule margin reasonable and logically distributed?

267. Is there an on-going process in place to monitor Service Lines project risks?

268. Were Service Lines project team members

involved in detailed estimating and scheduling?

269. Were stakeholders aware and supportive of the principles and practices of modern software estimation?

270. Are Service Lines project contact logs kept up to date?

271. Will the Service Lines project sponsor be involved in preliminary schedule reviews?

272. Does a documented Service Lines project organizational policy & plan (i.e. governance model) exist?

273. How relevant is this attribute to this Service Lines project or audit?

274. Sensitivity analysis?

275. Is there a formal set of procedures supporting Stakeholder Management?

276. Are software metrics formally captured, analyzed and used as a basis for other Service Lines project estimates?

2.11 Activity List: Service Lines

277. How much slack is available in the Service Lines project?

278. When will the work be performed?

279. Are the required resources available or need to be acquired?

280. What did not go as well?

281. What is the probability the Service Lines project can be completed in xx weeks?

282. What is the total time required to complete the Service Lines project if no delays occur?

283. Who will perform the work?

284. How do you determine the late start (LS) for each activity?

285. For other activities, how much delay can be tolerated?

286. What is the LF and LS for each activity?

287. What are you counting on?

288. Is there anything planned that does not need to be here?

289. How will it be performed?

290. What will be performed?

291. Where will it be performed?

292. What are the critical bottleneck activities?

293. What went well?

294. When do the individual activities need to start and finish?

2.12 Activity Attributes: Service Lines

295. What went wrong?

296. Activity: what is In the Bag?

297. How difficult will it be to complete specific activities on this Service Lines project?

298. How much activity detail is required?

299. Has management defined a definite timeframe for the turnaround or Service Lines project window?

300. Would you consider either of corresponding activities an outlier?

301. Can you re-assign any activities to another resource to resolve an over-allocation?

302. Have constraints been applied to the start and finish milestones for the phases?

303. Activity: fair or not fair?

304. Resource is assigned to?

305. Why?

306. Does your organization of the data change its meaning?

307. How many days do you need to complete the work scope with a limit of X number of resources?

308. What is missing?

309. What is the general pattern here?

310. What conclusions/generalizations can you draw from this?

311. Time for overtime?

312. What activity do you think you should spend the most time on?

2.13 Milestone List: Service Lines

313. Continuity, supply chain robustness?

314. What is your organizations history in doing similar activities?

315. Describe the concept of the technology, product or service that will be or has been developed. How will it be used?

316. What is the market for your technology, product or service?

317. How will the milestone be verified?

318. How late can the activity finish?

319. Milestone pages should display the UserID of the person who added the milestone. Does a report or query exist that provides this audit information?

320. Legislative effects?

321. Reliability of data, plan predictability?

322. What specific improvements did you make to the Service Lines project proposal since the previous time?

323. What background experience, skills, and strengths does the team bring to your organization?

324. When will the Service Lines project be complete?

325. Own known vulnerabilities?

326. Usps (unique selling points)?

327. How difficult will it be to do specific activities on this Service Lines project?

328. Environmental effects?

329. It is to be a narrative text providing the crucial aspects of your Service Lines project proposal answering what, who, how, when and where?

2.14 Network Diagram: Service Lines

330. If the Service Lines project network diagram cannot change and you have extra personnel resources, what is the BEST thing to do?

331. What are the tools?

332. What job or jobs precede it?

333. What are the Key Success Factors?

334. What controls the start and finish of a job?

335. What is the probability of completing the Service Lines project in less that xx days?

336. If x is long, what would be the completion time if you break x into two parallel parts of y weeks and z weeks?

337. What job or jobs could run concurrently?

338. Will crashing x weeks return more in benefits than it costs?

339. Where do schedules come from?

340. Review the logical flow of the network diagram. Take a look at which activities you have first and then sequence the activities. Do they make sense?

341. Where do you schedule uncertainty time?

342. What must be completed before an activity can be started?

343. Why must you schedule milestones, such as reviews, throughout the Service Lines project?

344. What job or jobs follow it?

345. What can be done concurrently?

346. What are the Major Administrative Issues?

347. Exercise: what is the probability that the Service Lines project duration will exceed xx weeks?

348. If a current contract exists, can you provide the vendor name, contract start, and contract expiration date?

2.15 Activity Resource Requirements: Service Lines

349. Why do you do that?

350. How many signatures do you require on a check and does this match what is in your policy and procedures?

351. Which logical relationship does the PDM use most often?

352. What are constraints that you might find during the Human Resource Planning process?

353. How do you handle petty cash?

354. Organizational Applicability?

355. Are there unresolved issues that need to be addressed?

356. Other support in specific areas?

357. When does monitoring begin?

358. Anything else?

359. Do you use tools like decomposition and rolling-wave planning to produce the activity list and other outputs?

360. What is the Work Plan Standard?

361. How do you manage time?

2.16 Resource Breakdown Structure: Service Lines

362. How can this help you with team building?

363. What defines a successful Service Lines project?

364. Who needs what information?

365. What is each stakeholders desired outcome for the Service Lines project?

366. What can you do to improve productivity?

367. What is the difference between % Complete and % work?

368. What defines a successful Service Lines project?

369. Which resource planning tool provides information on resource responsibility and accountability?

370. Who will use the system?

371. Who delivers the information?

372. Why is this important?

373. How should the information be delivered?

374. What is Service Lines project communication management?

375. What is the number one predictor of a groups productivity?

376. Why do you do it?

377. How difficult will it be to do specific activities on this Service Lines project?

378. Which resources should be in the resource pool?

379. Why time management?

2.17 Activity Duration Estimates: Service Lines

380. How does the job market and current state of the economy affect human resource management?

381. Does a process exist to identify individuals authorized to make certain decisions?

382. What is the duration of the critical path for this Service Lines project?

383. What is done after activity duration estimation?

384. How does Service Lines project integration management relate to the Service Lines project life cycle, stakeholders, and the other Service Lines project management knowledge areas?

385. What are key inputs and outputs of the software?

386. Does a process exist to identify Service Lines project roles, responsibilities and reporting relationships?

387. Why is outsourcing growing so rapidly?

388. What are the main processes included in Service Lines project quality management?

389. Do procedures exist describing how the Service Lines project scope will be managed?

390. Are expert judgment and historical information utilized to estimate activity duration?

391. What do you think the real problem was in this case?

392. Are procedures defined for calculating cost estimates?

393. What is the critical path for this Service Lines project and how long is it?

394. Does a process exist to formally recognize new Service Lines projects?

395. How many different communications channels does a Service Lines project team with six people have?

396. Consider the examples of poor quality in information technology Service Lines projects presented in the What Went Wrong?

397. Are training needs identified when resources do not have the required skills to complete Service Lines project activities?

398. Are activity dependencies documented?

2.18 Duration Estimating Worksheet: Service Lines

399. Is this operation cost effective?

400. Science = process: remember the scientific method?

401. What is an Average Service Lines project?

402. What is next?

403. Define the work as completely as possible. What work will be included in the Service Lines project?

404. When does your organization expect to be able to complete it?

405. Can the Service Lines project be constructed as planned?

406. What work will be included in the Service Lines project?

407. What utility impacts are there?

408. Why estimate costs?

409. Does the Service Lines project provide innovative ways for stakeholders to overcome obstacles or deliver better outcomes?

410. Do any colleagues have experience with your

organization and/or RFPs?

411. Is the Service Lines project responsive to community need?

412. What questions do you have?

413. Will the Service Lines project collaborate with the local community and leverage resources?

414. Value pocket identification & quantification what are value pockets?

2.19 Project Schedule: Service Lines

415. Why or why not?

416. Should you include sub-activities?

417. Why do you need schedules?

418. Did the Service Lines project come in under budget?

419. How much slack is available in the Service Lines project?

420. How many levels?

421. How effectively were issues able to be resolved without impacting the Service Lines project Schedule or Budget?

422. What is risk management?

423. Service Lines project work estimates Who is managing the work estimate quality of work tasks in the Service Lines project schedule?

424. Month Service Lines project take?

425. Your Service Lines project management plan results in a Service Lines project schedule that is too long. If the Service Lines project network diagram cannot change and you have extra personnel resources, what is the BEST thing to do?

426. It allows the Service Lines project to be delivered on schedule. How Do you Use Schedules?

427. Is Service Lines project work proceeding in accordance with the original Service Lines project schedule?

428. Have all Service Lines project delays been adequately accounted for, communicated to all stakeholders and adjustments made in overall Service Lines project schedule?

429. Is the Service Lines project schedule available for all Service Lines project team members to review?

430. Eliminate unnecessary activities. Are there activities that came from a template or previous Service Lines project that are not applicable on this phase of this Service Lines project?

431. Master Service Lines project schedule?

432. Are key risk mitigation strategies added to the Service Lines project schedule?

433. What is the difference?

2.20 Cost Management Plan: Service Lines

434. Service Lines project Objectives?

435. How relevant is this attribute to this Service Lines project or audit?

436. Is it possible to track all classes of Service Lines project work (e.g. scheduled, un-scheduled, defect repair, etc.)?

437. Have Service Lines project team accountabilities & responsibilities been clearly defined?

438. Have Service Lines project management standards and procedures been identified / established and documented?

439. Are cause and effect determined for risks when others occur?

440. The definition of the Service Lines project scope what needs to be accomplished?

441. Forecasts – how will the cost to complete the Service Lines project be forecast?

442. Contractors scope – how will contractors scope be defined when contracts are let?

443. Has a structured approach been used to break work effort into manageable components (WBS)?

444. Have activity relationships and interdependencies within tasks been adequately identified?

445. Is current scope of the Service Lines project substantially different than that originally defined?

446. Service Lines project definition & scope?

447. Why do you manage cost?

448. Is a stakeholder management plan in place that covers topics?

449. Does the resource management plan include a personnel development plan?

450. Are target dates established for each milestone deliverable?

451. What is the work breakdown structure for the Service Lines project?

2.21 Activity Cost Estimates: Service Lines

452. Are data needed on characteristics of care?

453. What is Service Lines project cost management?

454. Will you need to provide essential services information about activities?

455. Where can you get activity reports?

456. What defines a successful Service Lines project?

457. When do you enter into PPM?

458. What areas does the group agree are the biggest success on the Service Lines project?

459. What are the audit requirements?

460. How do you fund change orders?

461. How and when do you enter into Service Lines project Procurement Management?

462. How do you do activity recasts?

463. How do you manage cost?

464. Was it performed on time?

465. Does the activity serve a common type of

customer?

466. What were things that you did very well and want to do the same again on the next Service Lines project?

467. Were escalated issues resolved promptly?

468. Who & what determines the need for contracted services?

469. Measurable - are the targets measurable?

470. In which phase of the acquisition process cycle does source qualifications reside?

2.22 Cost Estimating Worksheet: Service Lines

471. Is it feasible to establish a control group arrangement?

472. How will the results be shared and to whom?

473. What additional Service Lines project(s) could be initiated as a result of this Service Lines project?

474. Is the Service Lines project responsive to community need?

475. Does the Service Lines project provide innovative ways for stakeholders to overcome obstacles or deliver better outcomes?

476. Identify the timeframe necessary to monitor progress and collect data to determine how the selected measure has changed?

477. What will others want?

478. What is the purpose of estimating?

479. What happens to any remaining funds not used?

480. What is the estimated labor cost today based upon this information?

481. Ask: are others positioned to know, are others credible, and will others cooperate?

482. Will the Service Lines project collaborate with the local community and leverage resources?

483. What can be included?

484. Who is best positioned to know and assist in identifying corresponding factors?

485. Can a trend be established from historical performance data on the selected measure and are the criteria for using trend analysis or forecasting methods met?

486. What costs are to be estimated?

487. What info is needed?

2.23 Cost Baseline: Service Lines

488. What is your organizations history in doing similar tasks?

489. Does the suggested change request seem to represent a necessary enhancement to the product?

490. On budget?

491. If you sold 10x widgets on a day, what would the affect on profits be?

492. On time?

493. Has the Service Lines project documentation been archived or otherwise disposed as described in the Service Lines project communication plan?

494. What strengths do you have?

495. Does the suggested change request represent a desired enhancement to the products functionality?

496. Has the documentation relating to operation and maintenance of the product(s) or service(s) been delivered to, and accepted by, operations management?

497. Pcs for your new business. what would the life cycle costs be?

498. Have the resources used by the Service Lines project been reassigned to other units or Service

Lines projects?

499. Has the Service Lines projected annual cost to operate and maintain the product(s) or service(s) been approved and funded?

500. Review your risk triggers -have your risks changed?

501. Will the Service Lines project fail if the change request is not executed?

502. Escalation criteria met?

503. What can go wrong?

504. Where do changes come from?

505. Are you meeting with your team regularly?

2.24 Quality Management Plan: Service Lines

506. Sampling part of task?

507. Who gets results of work?

508. What does it do for you (or to me)?

509. What are your organizations current levels and trends for the already stated measures related to financial and marketplace performance?

510. How does your organization manage training and evaluate its effectiveness?

511. What is the Quality Management Plan?

512. Does the program use modeling in the permitting or decision-making processes?

513. Were there any deficiencies / issues identified in the prior years self-assessment?

514. Are there processes in place to ensure internal consistency between the source code components?

515. Diagrams and tables to account for complex concepts and increase overall readability?

516. How do you check in-coming sample material?

517. Does a documented Service Lines project

organizational policy & plan (i.e. governance model) exist?

518. What are your organizations key processes (product, service, business, and support)?

519. What are your key performance measures/ indicators for tracking progress relative to your action plans?

520. Why quality management?

521. How do you ensure that protocols are up to date?

522. Who is responsible?

523. How does your organization manage work to promote cooperation, individual initiative, innovation, flexibility, communications, and knowledge/skill sharing across work units?

524. How are senior leaders, employees, and your organization involved in supporting the community?

525. Is there a Quality Management Plan?

2.25 Quality Metrics: Service Lines

526. Was the overall quality better or worse than previous products?

527. There are many reasons to shore up quality-related metrics, and what metrics are important?

528. Subjective quality component: customer satisfaction, how do you measure it?

529. Why is now the time for quality metrics?

530. What level of statistical confidence do you use?

531. How do you measure?

532. How exactly do you define when differences exist?

533. How should customers provide input?

534. Do the operators focus on determining; is there anything you need to worry about?

535. Are applicable standards referenced and available?

536. Product Availability ?

537. Do you know how much profit a 10% decrease in waste would generate?

538. What metrics are important and most beneficial

to measure?

539. What group is empowered to define quality requirements?

540. Were quality attributes reported?

541. What documentation is required?

542. How is it being measured?

543. What about still open problems?

544. Is there a set of procedures to capture, analyze and act on quality metrics?

545. What can manufacturing professionals do to ensure quality is seen as an integral part of the entire product lifecycle?

2.26 Process Improvement Plan: Service Lines

546. Are there forms and procedures to collect and record the data?

547. Have the frequency of collection and the points in the process where measurements will be made been determined?

548. If a process improvement framework is being used, which elements will help the problems and goals listed?

549. What is quality and how will you ensure it?

550. Does your process ensure quality?

551. To elicit goal statements, do you ask a question such as, What do you want to achieve?

552. Where are you now?

553. Where do you want to be?

554. Are you following the quality standards?

555. What actions are needed to address the problems and achieve the goals?

556. Modeling current processes is great, and will you ever see a return on that investment?

557. Everyone agrees on what process improvement is, right?

558. Have the supporting tools been developed or acquired?

559. What is the return on investment?

560. What lessons have you learned so far?

561. Who should prepare the process improvement action plan?

562. How do you manage quality?

563. Where do you focus?

2.27 Responsibility Assignment Matrix: Service Lines

564. Is the entire contract planned in time-phased control accounts to the extent practicable?

565. Service Lines projected economic escalation?

566. Do work packages consist of discrete tasks which are adequately described?

567. When performing is split among two or more roles, is the work clearly defined so that the efforts are coordinated and the communication is clear?

568. Are management actions taken to reduce indirect costs when there are significant adverse variances?

569. Major functional areas of contract effort?

570. Does the contractors system identify work accomplishment against the schedule plan?

571. Do you need to convince people that its well worth the time and effort?

572. Too many is: do all the identified roles need to be routinely informed or only in exceptional circumstances?

573. Past experience – the person or the group worked at something similar in the past?

574. Most people let you know when others re too busy, and are others really too busy?

575. No rs: if a task has no one listed as responsible, who is getting the job done?

576. Budgeted cost for work scheduled?

577. What travel needed?

578. Are work packages assigned to performing organizations?

579. Is the anticipated (firm and potential) business base Service Lines projected in a rational, consistent manner?

580. Do all the identified groups or people really need to be consulted?

581. Are the actual costs used for variance analysis reconcilable with data from the accounting system?

582. Are people afraid to let you know when others are under allocated?

2.28 Roles and Responsibilities: Service Lines

583. Are your policies supportive of a culture of quality data?

584. Do the values and practices inherent in the culture of your organization foster or hinder the process?

585. Concern: where are you limited or have no authority, where you can not influence?

586. What should you do now to prepare for your career 5+ years from now?

587. What expectations were met?

588. What should you do now to ensure that you are meeting all expectations of your current position?

589. Are Service Lines project team roles and responsibilities identified and documented?

590. Who is responsible for implementation activities and where will the functions, roles and responsibilities be defined?

591. Does the team have access to and ability to use data analysis tools?

592. Where are you most strong as a supervisor?

593. What should you highlight for improvement?

594. Who is involved?

595. Are Service Lines project team roles and responsibilities identified and documented?

596. Do you take the time to clearly define roles and responsibilities on Service Lines project tasks?

597. Who: who is involved?

598. What specific behaviors did you observe?

599. Authority: what areas/Service Lines projects in your work do you have the authority to decide upon and act on the already stated decisions?

600. Was the expectation clearly communicated?

601. Accountabilities: what are the roles and responsibilities of individual team members?

602. Implementation of actions: Who are the responsible units?

2.29 Human Resource Management Plan: Service Lines

603. Have external dependencies been captured in the schedule?

604. Quality of people required to meet the forecast needs of the department?

605. Are status reports received per the Service Lines project Plan?

606. Were Service Lines project team members involved in detailed estimating and scheduling?

607. Have Service Lines project management standards and procedures been identified / established and documented?

608. Are people motivated to meet the current and future challenges?

609. Are there dependencies with other initiatives or Service Lines projects?

610. Is a pmo (Service Lines project management office) in place and provide oversight to the Service Lines project?

611. Identify who is needed on the core Service Lines project team to complete Service Lines project deliverables and achieve its goals and objectives. What skills, knowledge and experiences are required?

612. Have Service Lines project team accountabilities & responsibilities been clearly defined?

613. How can below standard performers be guided/ developed to upgrade performance?

614. Is your organization human?

615. Are adequate resources provided for the quality assurance function?

616. How will the Service Lines project manage expectations & meet needs and requirements?

617. Who will be impacted (both positively and negatively) as a result of or during the execution of this Service Lines project?

618. Are assumptions being identified, recorded, analyzed, qualified and closed?

619. How are superior performers differentiated from average performers?

620. Have adequate resources been provided by management to ensure Service Lines project success?

621. Are mitigation strategies identified?

2.30 Communications Management Plan: Service Lines

622. Do you have members of your team responsible for certain stakeholders?

623. Is there an important stakeholder who is actively opposed and will not receive messages?

624. Who is involved as you identify stakeholders?

625. What communications method?

626. What steps can you take for a positive relationship?

627. Who needs to know and how much?

628. What is the stakeholders level of authority?

629. Do you feel more overwhelmed by stakeholders?

630. Conflict resolution -which method when?

631. Who is the stakeholder?

632. Which stakeholders can influence others?

633. Why do you manage communications?

634. What are the interrelationships?

635. Are others needed?

636. How were corresponding initiatives successful?

637. What to learn?

638. Do you prepare stakeholder engagement plans?

639. What does the stakeholder need from the team?

640. Do you ask; can you recommend others for you to talk with about this initiative?

641. Where do team members get information?

2.31 Risk Management Plan: Service Lines

642. How can you fix it?

643. How quickly does each item need to be resolved?

644. Prioritized components/features?

645. Is there additional information that would make you more confident about your analysis?

646. How risk averse are you?

647. Is security a central objective?

648. Maximize short-term return on investment?

649. What is the cost to the Service Lines project if it does occur?

650. Can the risk be avoided by choosing a different alternative?

651. What is the likelihood that your organization would accept responsibility for the risk?

652. What should be done with non-critical risks?

653. Where do risks appear in the business phases?

654. Havent software Service Lines projects been late before?

655. Premium on reliability of product?

656. Are the required plans included, such as nonstructural flood risk management plans?

657. How well were you able to manage your risk before?

658. What things might go wrong?

659. Are you on schedule?

660. People risk -are people with appropriate skills available to help complete the Service Lines project?

661. Are requirements fully understood by the software engineering team and customers?

2.32 Risk Register: Service Lines

662. Who is going to do it?

663. What would the impact to the Service Lines project objectives be should the risk arise?

664. What are the main aims, objectives of the policy, strategy, or service and the intended outcomes?

665. Risk probability and impact: how will the probabilities and impacts of risk items be assessed?

666. What is the reason for current performance gaps and do the risks and opportunities identified previously account for this?

667. Do you require further engagement?

668. Who needs to know about this?

669. How could corresponding Risk affect the Service Lines project in terms of cost and schedule?

670. Does the evidence highlight any areas to advance opportunities or foster good relations. If yes what steps will be taken?

671. Technology risk -is the Service Lines project technically feasible?

672. Risk documentation: what reporting formats and processes will be used for risk management activities?

673. What action, if any, has been taken to respond to the risk?

674. What is your current and future risk profile?

675. User involvement: do you have the right users?

676. How are risks graded?

677. Are corrective measures implemented as planned?

678. Why would you develop a risk register?

679. What has changed since the last period?

680. How is a Community Risk Register created?

2.33 Probability and Impact Assessment: Service Lines

681. Which of corresponding risk factors can be avoided altogether?

682. Are the risk data timely and relevant?

683. Has something like this been done before?

684. Do end-users have realistic expectations?

685. Are the facilities, expertise, resources, and management know-how available to handle the situation?

686. How is risk handled within this Service Lines project organization?

687. How would you assess the risk management process in the Service Lines project?

688. What risks does the employee encounter?

689. Is the technology to be built new to your organization?

690. Risks should be identified during which phase of Service Lines project management life cycle?

691. Do you manage the process through use of metrics?

692. Will there be an increase in the political conservatism?

693. What are the chances the risk event will occur?

694. Anticipated volatility of the requirements?

695. My Service Lines project leader has suddenly left your organization, what do you do?

696. Costs associated with late delivery or a defective product?

697. Is the customer willing to establish rapid communication links with the developer?

698. Have top software and customer managers formally committed to support the Service Lines project?

699. Has the need for the Service Lines project been properly established?

700. What are its business ethics?

2.34 Probability and Impact Matrix: Service Lines

701. Have top software and customer managers formally committed to support the Service Lines project?

702. What risks were tracked?

703. How well were you able to manage your risk?

704. Were there any Service Lines projects similar to this one in existence?

705. Are team members trained in the use of the tools?

706. Do you know the order of planning yet?

707. Do you use any methods to analyze risks?

708. Is the number of people on the Service Lines project team adequate to do the job?

709. What are the channels available for distribution to the customer?

710. Who should be notified of the occurrence of each of the risk indicators?

711. Management -what contingency plans do you have if the risk becomes a reality?

712. What are the levels of understanding of the future users of this technology?

713. Can you stabilize dynamic risk factors?

714. Several experts are offsite, and wish to be included. How can this be done?

715. Does the customer have a solid idea of what is required?

716. Who are the owners?

717. Are there new risks that mitigation strategies might introduce?

718. Which is an input to the risk management process?

719. What is the likelihood?

2.35 Risk Data Sheet: Service Lines

720. How do you handle product safely?

721. What are you here for (Mission)?

722. What was measured?

723. What can happen?

724. What actions can be taken to eliminate or remove risk?

725. Is the data sufficiently specified in terms of the type of failure being analyzed, and its frequency or probability?

726. What can you do?

727. Will revised controls lead to tolerable risk levels?

728. Type of risk identified?

729. What if client refuses?

730. If it happens, what are the consequences?

731. What were the Causes that contributed?

732. Are new hazards created?

733. What is the chance that it will happen?

734. What are your core values?

735. What is the likelihood of it happening?

736. How can hazards be reduced?

737. How reliable is the data source?

738. Has the most cost-effective solution been chosen?

2.36 Procurement Management Plan: Service Lines

739. Are the budget estimates reasonable?

740. Has your organization readiness assessment been conducted?

741. Based on your Service Lines project communication management plan, what worked well?

742. Is there a set of procedures defining the scope, procedures, and deliverables defining quality control?

743. Is there a procurement management plan in place?

744. Is the current scope of the Service Lines project substantially different than that originally defined?

745. Does a documented Service Lines project organizational policy & plan (i.e. governance model) exist?

746. Are quality metrics defined?

747. Have the key elements of a coherent Service Lines project management strategy been established?

748. Has a provision been made to reassess Service Lines project risks at various Service Lines project stages?

749. Are the Service Lines project team members located locally to the users/stakeholders?

750. Are the Service Lines project plans updated on a frequent basis?

751. Are updated Service Lines project time & resource estimates reasonable based on the current Service Lines project stage?

752. What is the last item a Service Lines project manager must do to finalize Service Lines project close-out?

753. Was an original risk assessment/risk management plan completed?

754. Are meeting minutes captured and sent out after meetings?

755. Were Service Lines project team members involved in detailed estimating and scheduling?

2.37 Source Selection Criteria: Service Lines

756. Do you have a plan to document consensus results including disposition of any disagreement by individual evaluators?

757. What are the special considerations for preaward debriefings?

758. Are responses to considerations adequate?

759. What should a DRFP include?

760. Can you prevent comparison of proposals?

761. Do you consider all weaknesses, significant weaknesses, and deficiencies?

762. When is it appropriate to issue a Draft Request for Proposal (DRFP)?

763. Are considerations anticipated?

764. What source selection software is your team using?

765. When and what information can be considered with offerors regarding past performance?

766. Are they compliant with all technical requirements?

767. Do proposed hours support content and schedule?

768. Is the offeror pricing what is technically proposed?

769. Have all evaluators been trained?

770. Is experience evaluated?

771. How do you facilitate evaluation against published criteria?

772. How do you encourage efficiency and consistency?

773. Do you prepare an independent cost estimate?

774. In the technical/management area, what criteria do you use to determine the final evaluation ratings?

775. Are types/quantities of material, facilities appropriate?

2.38 Stakeholder Management Plan: Service Lines

776. Are stakeholders aware and supportive of the principles and practices of modern software estimation?

777. Have the procedures for identifying budget variances been followed?

778. Have all team members been part of identifying risks?

779. What training requirements are there based upon the required skills and resources?

780. Is it standard practice to formally commit stakeholders to the Service Lines project via agreements?

781. Who is responsible for the post implementation review process?

782. What is positive about the current process?

783. How are you doing/what can be done better?

784. Are communication systems currently in place appropriate?

785. Does the business case include how the Service Lines project aligns with your organizations strategic goals & objectives?

786. Who will be responsible for managing and maintaining the Issues Register?

787. Is the assigned Service Lines project manager a PMP (Certified Service Lines project manager) and experienced?

788. Is Service Lines project status reviewed with the steering and executive teams at appropriate intervals?

789. Are there procedures in place to effectively manage interdependencies with other Service Lines projects / systems?

790. Do Service Lines project managers participating in the Service Lines project know the Service Lines projects true status first hand?

791. Is there an issues management plan in place?

2.39 Change Management Plan: Service Lines

792. What are the dependencies?

793. Has a training need analysis been carried out?

794. Who should be involved in developing a change management strategy?

795. Are there resource implications for your communications strategy?

796. What new roles are needed?

797. Who will fund the training?

798. Has the relevant business unit been notified of installation and support requirements?

799. What work practices will be affected?

800. What new competencies will be required for the roles?

801. What are the training strategies?

802. Who might present the most resistance?

803. What risks may occur upfront, during implementation and after implementation?

804. How frequently should you repeat the message?

805. Has the training provider been established?

806. How will you deal with anger about the restricting of communications due to confidentiality considerations?

807. How prevalent is Resistance to Change?

808. Is there a need for new relationships to be built?

809. Why is it important?

810. When should a given message be communicated?

811. Have the approved procedures and policies been published?

3.0 Executing Process Group: Service Lines

812. Does the case present a realistic scenario?

813. What are the critical steps involved in selecting measures and initiatives?

814. What are deliverables of your Service Lines project?

815. How do you enter durations, link tasks, and view critical path information?

816. Are the necessary foundations in place to ensure the sustainability of the results of the programme?

817. Do schedule issues conflicts?

818. What areas were overlooked on this Service Lines project?

819. What are the key components of the Service Lines project communications plan?

820. What are the main types of goods and services being outsourced?

821. Will outside resources be needed to help?

822. Contingency planning. if a risk event occurs, what will you do?

823. What factors are contributing to progress or delay in the achievement of products and results?

824. What is the product of your Service Lines project?

825. Does the Service Lines project team have enough people to execute the Service Lines project plan?

826. When do you share the scorecard with managers?

827. When will the Service Lines project be done?

828. How well did the chosen processes fit the needs of the Service Lines project?

829. Mitigate. what will you do to minimize the impact should a risk event occur?

830. Do the products created live up to the necessary quality?

3.1 Team Member Status Report: Service Lines

831. How will resource planning be done?

832. Why is it to be done?

833. Are the products of your organizations Service Lines projects meeting customers objectives?

834. How does this product, good, or service meet the needs of the Service Lines project and your organization as a whole?

835. What specific interest groups do you have in place?

836. Will the staff do training or is that done by a third party?

837. How much risk is involved?

838. Are the attitudes of staff regarding Service Lines project work improving?

839. Do you have an Enterprise Service Lines project Management Office (EPMO)?

840. How it is to be done?

841. Does your organization have the means (staff, money, contract, etc.) to produce or to acquire the product, good, or service?

842. When a teams productivity and success depend on collaboration and the efficient flow of information, what generally fails them?

843. Are your organizations Service Lines projects more successful over time?

844. Is there evidence that staff is taking a more professional approach toward management of your organizations Service Lines projects?

845. Does every department have to have a Service Lines project Manager on staff?

846. Does the product, good, or service already exist within your organization?

847. The problem with Reward & Recognition Programs is that the truly deserving people all too often get left out. How can you make it practical?

848. What is to be done?

849. How can you make it practical?

3.2 Change Request: Service Lines

850. What can be filed?

851. Why do you want to have a change control system?

852. What are the duties of the change control team?

853. Has your address changed?

854. Does the schedule include Service Lines project management time and change request analysis time?

855. When to submit a change request?

856. Has the change been highlighted and documented in the CSCI?

857. Will there be a change request form in use?

858. What are the Impacts to your organization?

859. What must be taken into consideration when introducing change control programs?

860. What are the basic mechanics of the Change Advisory Board (CAB)?

861. When do you create a change request?

862. Describe how modifications, enhancements, defects and/or deficiencies shall be notified (e.g. Problem Reports, Change Requests etc) and

managed. Detail warranty and/or maintenance periods?

863. How does a team identify the discrete elements of a configuration?

864. How many times must the change be modified or presented to the change control board before it is approved?

865. Can static requirements change attributes like the size of the change be used to predict reliability in execution?

866. What kind of information about the change request needs to be captured?

867. What is a Change Request Form?

868. What type of changes does change control take into account?

3.3 Change Log: Service Lines

869. Is this a mandatory replacement?

870. Is the requested change request a result of changes in other Service Lines project(s)?

871. How does this change affect scope?

872. Do the described changes impact on the integrity or security of the system?

873. Is the change request open, closed or pending?

874. When was the request approved?

875. Who initiated the change request?

876. Is the change request within Service Lines project scope?

877. How does this relate to the standards developed for specific business processes?

878. How does this change affect the timeline of the schedule?

879. Is the change backward compatible without limitations?

880. When was the request submitted?

881. Is the submitted change a new change or a modification of a previously approved change?

882. Will the Service Lines project fail if the change request is not executed?

883. Should a more thorough impact analysis be conducted?

3.4 Decision Log: Service Lines

884. How do you know when you are achieving it?

885. Behaviors; what are guidelines that the team has identified that will assist them with getting the most out of team meetings?

886. How does the use a Decision Support System influence the strategies/tactics or costs?

887. Adversarial environment. is your opponent open to a non-traditional workflow, or will it likely challenge anything you do?

888. At what point in time does loss become unacceptable?

889. Is your opponent open to a non-traditional workflow, or will it likely challenge anything you do?

890. What was the rationale for the decision?

891. How consolidated and comprehensive a story can you tell by capturing currently available incident data in a central location and through a log of key decisions during an incident?

892. Linked to original objective?

893. What is the average size of your matters in an applicable measurement?

894. It becomes critical to track and periodically revisit

both operational effectiveness; Are you noticing all that you need to, and are you interpreting what you see effectively?

895. With whom was the decision shared or considered?

896. What is the line where eDiscovery ends and document review begins?

897. Decision-making process; how will the team make decisions?

898. Which variables make a critical difference?

899. What eDiscovery problem or issue did your organization set out to fix or make better?

900. What is your overall strategy for quality control / quality assurance procedures?

901. Does anything need to be adjusted?

902. How does an increasing emphasis on cost containment influence the strategies and tactics used?

903. What alternatives/risks were considered?

3.5 Quality Audit: Service Lines

904. What does an analysis of your organizations staff profile suggest in terms of its planning, and how is this being addressed?

905. It is inappropriate to seek information about the Audit Panels preliminary views including questions like why do you ask that?

906. How does your organization know that its teaching activities (and staff learning) are effectively and constructively enhanced by its activities?

907. How does your organization know that its system for examining work done is appropriately effective and constructive?

908. How does your organization know that its quality of teaching is appropriately effective and constructive?

909. How does your organization know that its system for inducting new staff to maximize workplace contributions are appropriately effective and constructive?

910. Are the intentions consistent with external obligations (such as applicable laws)?

911. How does your organization know that the support for its staff is appropriately effective and constructive?

912. What mechanisms exist for identification of staff development needs?

913. Is the reports overall tone appropriate?

914. Are the policies and processes, as set out in the Quality Audit Manual, properly applied?

915. How does your organization know that the range and quality of its social and recreational services and facilities are appropriately effective and constructive in meeting the needs of staff?

916. Are the review comments incorporated?

917. How does your organization know that its system for commercializing research outputs is appropriately effective and constructive?

918. How does your organization know that its systems for assisting staff with career planning and employment placements are appropriately effective and constructive?

919. Are training programs documented?

920. What are you trying to accomplish with this audit?

921. How does your organization know that the system for managing its facilities is appropriately effective and constructive?

922. How does your organization know that its Mission, Vision and Values Statements are appropriate and effectively guiding your organization?

3.6 Team Directory: Service Lines

923. Process decisions: are there any statutory or regulatory issues relevant to the timely execution of work?

924. Have you decided when to celebrate the Service Lines projects completion date?

925. Contract requirements complied with?

926. What are you going to deliver or accomplish?

927. Process decisions: is work progressing on schedule and per contract requirements?

928. Decisions: what could be done better to improve the quality of the constructed product?

929. Process decisions: which organizational elements and which individuals will be assigned management functions?

930. Process decisions: do job conditions warrant additional actions to collect job information and document on-site activity?

931. Decisions: is the most suitable form of contract being used?

932. Who will write the meeting minutes and distribute?

933. How does the team resolve conflicts and ensure

tasks are completed?

934. Days from the time the issue is identified?

935. How will you accomplish and manage the objectives?

936. When does information need to be distributed?

937. Who will be the stakeholders on your next Service Lines project?

938. Process decisions: do invoice amounts match accepted work in place?

939. Process decisions: are all start-up, turn over and close out requirements of the contract satisfied?

940. Do purchase specifications and configurations match requirements?

941. Is construction on schedule?

3.7 Team Operating Agreement: Service Lines

942. Did you determine the technology methods that best match the messages to be communicated?

943. Must your team members rely on the expertise of other members to complete tasks?

944. Have you established procedures that team members can follow to work effectively together, such as a team operating agreement?

945. What are the current caseload numbers in the unit?

946. Are there more than two national cultures represented by your team?

947. Do you prevent individuals from dominating the meeting?

948. Do you solicit member feedback about meetings and what would make them better?

949. Why does your organization want to participate in teaming?

950. Resource allocation: how will individual team members account for time and expenses, and how will this be allocated in the team budget?

951. Seconds for members to respond?

952. To whom do you deliver your services?

953. Do you send out the agenda and meeting materials in advance?

954. Do you ensure that all participants know how to use the required technology?

955. Do you vary your voice pace, tone and pitch to engage participants and gain involvement?

956. Do you record meetings for the already stated unable to attend?

957. What is the number of cases currently teamed?

958. What is your unique contribution to your organization?

959. What types of accommodations will be formulated and put in place for sustaining the team?

960. What is group supervision?

961. Have you set the goals and objectives of the team?

3.8 Team Performance Assessment: Service Lines

962. To what degree are the members clear on what they are individually responsible for and what they are jointly responsible for?

963. When a reviewer complains about method variance, what is the essence of the complaint?

964. To what degree are staff involved as partners in the improvement process?

965. To what degree can the team measure progress against specific goals?

966. If you have received criticism from reviewers that your work suffered from method variance, what was the circumstance?

967. To what degree do the goals specify concrete team work products?

968. To what degree do team members frequently explore the teams purpose and its implications?

969. To what degree can all members engage in open and interactive considerations?

970. Does more radicalness mean more perceived benefits?

971. To what degree will team members, individually

and collectively, commit time to help themselves and others learn and develop skills?

972. What is method variance?

973. Can familiarity breed backup?

974. Is there a particular method of data analysis that you would recommend as a means of demonstrating that method variance is not of great concern for a given dataset?

975. Can team performance be reliably measured in simulator and live exercises using the same assessment tool?

976. To what degree does the teams approach to its work allow for modification and improvement over time?

977. To what degree does the teams work approach provide opportunity for members to engage in fact-based problem solving?

978. When does the medium matter?

979. To what degree do team members understand one anothers roles and skills?

980. To what degree do team members feel that the purpose of the team is important, if not exciting?

981. Do you promptly inform members about major developments that may affect them?

3.9 Team Member Performance Assessment: Service Lines

982. How is the timing of assessments organized (e.g., pre/post-test, single point during training, multiple reassessment during training)?

983. What are best practices in use for the performance measurement system?

984. To what degree do members articulate the goals beyond the team membership?

985. What kinds of performance factors / elements do you use?

986. What steps have you taken to improve performance?

987. How are performance measures and associated incentives developed?

988. What are best practices for delivering and developing training evaluations to maximize the benefits of leveraging emerging technologies?

989. What evaluation results do you have?

990. To what degree can team members frequently and easily communicate with one another?

991. Does adaptive training work?

992. How do you implement Cost Reduction?

993. Does the rater (supervisor) have the authority or responsibility to tell an employee that the employees performance is unsatisfactory?

994. What happens if a team member receives a Rating of Unsatisfactory?

995. Can your organization rate by exception and assume that most employees are performing at an acceptable level?

996. What are the basic principles and objectives of performance measurement and assessment?

997. What stakeholders must be involved in the development and oversight of the performance plan?

998. What is needed for effective data teams?

999. Are the draft goals SMART ?

3.10 Issue Log: Service Lines

1000. What approaches to you feel are the best ones to use?

1001. Do you often overlook a key stakeholder or stakeholder group?

1002. Why not more evaluators?

1003. Are the stakeholders getting the information they need, are they consulted, are concerns addressed?

1004. Why do you manage human resources?

1005. Is the issue log kept in a safe place?

1006. Are they needed?

1007. Who are the members of the governing body?

1008. Can you think of other people who might have concerns or interests?

1009. How do you reply to this question; you am new here and managing this major program. How do you suggest you build your network?

1010. Is access to the Issue Log controlled?

1011. How were past initiatives successful?

1012. Do you feel a register helps?

1013. What approaches do you use?

1014. Are you constantly rushing from meeting to meeting?

1015. What steps can you take for positive relationships?

4.0 Monitoring and Controlling Process Group: Service Lines

1016. Is there undesirable impact on staff or resources?

1017. Is the schedule for the set products being met?

1018. Are the services being delivered?

1019. Is there adequate validation on required fields?

1020. How is agile portfolio management done?

1021. Do the partners have sufficient financial capacity to keep up the benefits produced by the programme?

1022. Were sponsors and decision makers available when needed outside regularly scheduled meetings?

1023. What communication items need improvement?

1024. How is agile program management done?

1025. How can you make your needs known?

1026. How well did the chosen processes fit the needs of the Service Lines project?

1027. What input will you be required to provide the Service Lines project team?

1028. How well did the chosen processes produce the expected results?

1029. Is the verbiage used appropriate and understandable?

1030. Key stakeholders to work with. How many potential communications channels exist on the Service Lines project?

1031. Were decisions made in a timely manner?

1032. How do you monitor progress?

4.1 Project Performance Report: Service Lines

1033. How is the data used?

1034. To what degree does the information network communicate information relevant to the task?

1035. What is the degree to which rules govern information exchange between individuals within your organization?

1036. To what degree do all members feel responsible for all agreed-upon measures?

1037. To what degree does the teams purpose contain themes that are particularly meaningful and memorable?

1038. To what degree will the approach capitalize on and enhance the skills of all team members in a manner that takes into consideration other demands on members of the team?

1039. To what degree does the funding match the requirement?

1040. To what degree are the goals ambitious?

1041. To what degree does the task meet individual needs?

1042. To what degree is there centralized control of

information sharing?

1043. To what degree do team members articulate the teams work approach?

1044. To what degree do the structures of the formal organization motivate taskrelevant behavior and facilitate task completion?

1045. To what degree can team members meet frequently enough to accomplish the teams ends?

1046. To what degree is the information network consistent with the structure of the formal organization?

4.2 Variance Analysis: Service Lines

1047. What types of services and expense are shared between business segments?

1048. What can be the cause of an increase in costs?

1049. Are all elements of indirect expense identified to overhead cost budgets of Service Lines projections?

1050. Does the scheduling system identify in a timely manner the status of work?

1051. Does the contractors system include procedures for measuring the performance of critical subcontractors?

1052. How are variances affected by multiple material and labor categories?

1053. What is the expected future profitability of each customer?

1054. Is all contract work included in the CWBS?

1055. What is the performance to date and material commitment?

1056. Are there externalities from having some customers, even if they are unprofitable in the short run?

1057. How do you identify and isolate causes of

favorable and unfavorable cost and schedule variances?

1058. Budget versus actual. how does the monthly budget compare to actual experience?

1059. What is the dollar amount of the fluctuation?

1060. Are there changes in the direct base to which overhead costs are allocated?

1061. Are overhead cost budgets established for each department which has authority to incur overhead costs?

1062. Favorable or unfavorable variance?

1063. Who are responsible for overhead performance control of related costs?

1064. Are all budgets assigned to control accounts?

1065. Are records maintained to show how undistributed budgets are controlled?

1066. What was the cause of the increase in costs?

4.3 Earned Value Status: Service Lines

1067. Where are your problem areas?

1068. Validation is a process of ensuring that the developed system will actually achieve the stakeholders desired outcomes; Are you building the right product? What do you validate?

1069. Where is evidence-based earned value in your organization reported?

1070. Verification is a process of ensuring that the developed system satisfies the stakeholders agreements and specifications; Are you building the product right? What do you verify?

1071. Are you hitting your Service Lines projects targets?

1072. If earned value management (EVM) is so good in determining the true status of a Service Lines project and Service Lines project its completion, why is it that hardly any one uses it in information systems related Service Lines projects?

1073. What is the unit of forecast value?

1074. How does this compare with other Service Lines projects?

1075. Earned value can be used in almost any Service Lines project situation and in almost any Service Lines project environment. it may be used on large Service

Lines projects, medium sized Service Lines projects, tiny Service Lines projects (in cut-down form), complex and simple Service Lines projects and in any market sector. some people, of course, know all about earned value, they have used it for years - but perhaps not as effectively as they could have?

1076. How much is it going to cost by the finish?

1077. When is it going to finish?

4.4 Risk Audit: Service Lines

1078. What responsibilities for quality, errors, and outcomes have been delegated to staff (or others) without adequate oversight?

1079. Tradeoff: how much risk can be tolerated and still deliver the products where they need to be?

1080. Can analytical tests provide evidence that is as strong as evidence from traditional substantive tests?

1081. Are you meeting your legal, regulatory and compliance requirements - if not, why not?

1082. Assessing risk with analytical procedures: do systemsthinking tools help auditors focus on diagnostic patterns?

1083. Does your organization communicate regularly and effectively with its members?

1084. Does your organization meet the terms of any contracts with which it is involved?

1085. Do all coaches/instructors/leaders have appropriate and current accreditation?

1086. Have you worked with the customer in the past?

1087. Have all involved been advised of any obligations they have to sponsors?

1088. Are risk management strategies documented?

1089. What are the benefits of a Enterprise wide approach to Risk Management?

1090. Do you have a mechanism for managing change?

1091. Are auditors able to effectively apply more soft evidence found in the risk-assessment process with the results of more tangible audit evidence found through more substantive testing?

1092. Auditor independence: a burdensome constraint or a core value?

1093. Do your financial policies and procedures ensure that each step in financial handling (receipt, recording, banking, reporting) is not completed by one person?

1094. If applicable; does the software interface with new or unproven hardware or unproven vendor products?

1095. Have customers been involved fully in the definition of requirements?

1096. How do you govern assets?

4.5 Contractor Status Report: Service Lines

1097. How does the proposed individual meet each requirement?

1098. Are there contractual transfer concerns?

1099. What was the final actual cost?

1100. What was the actual budget or estimated cost for your organizations services?

1101. Describe how often regular updates are made to the proposed solution. Are corresponding regular updates included in the standard maintenance plan?

1102. Who can list a Service Lines project as organization experience, your organization or a previous employee of your organization?

1103. If applicable; describe your standard schedule for new software version releases. Are new software version releases included in the standard maintenance plan?

1104. How is risk transferred?

1105. How long have you been using the services?

1106. What are the minimum and optimal bandwidth requirements for the proposed solution?

1107. What process manages the contracts?

1108. What was the budget or estimated cost for your organizations services?

1109. What is the average response time for answering a support call?

1110. What was the overall budget or estimated cost?

4.6 Formal Acceptance: Service Lines

1111. What function(s) does it fill or meet?

1112. Was the Service Lines project goal achieved?

1113. Does it do what client said it would?

1114. Do you perform formal acceptance or burn-in tests?

1115. Was the sponsor/customer satisfied?

1116. How does your team plan to obtain formal acceptance on your Service Lines project?

1117. Do you buy-in installation services?

1118. Do you buy pre-configured systems or build your own configuration?

1119. What was done right?

1120. General estimate of the costs and times to complete the Service Lines project?

1121. What features, practices, and processes proved to be strengths or weaknesses?

1122. What is the Acceptance Management Process?

1123. Did the Service Lines project manager and team act in a professional and ethical manner?

1124. Was the Service Lines project work done on time, within budget, and according to specification?

1125. Who would use it?

1126. Does it do what Service Lines project team said it would?

1127. Did the Service Lines project achieve its MOV?

1128. What lessons were learned about your Service Lines project management methodology?

1129. Have all comments been addressed?

1130. Was business value realized?

5.0 Closing Process Group: Service Lines

1131. Is this an updated Service Lines project Proposal Document?

1132. Did the Service Lines project team have the right skills?

1133. Was the user/client satisfied with the end product?

1134. How well did the team follow the chosen processes?

1135. Were risks identified and mitigated?

1136. What is the Service Lines project name and date of completion?

1137. Are there funding or time constraints?

1138. How dependent is the Service Lines project on other Service Lines projects or work efforts?

1139. Is this a follow-on to a previous Service Lines project?

1140. What areas were overlooked on this Service Lines project?

1141. Did you do what you said you were going to do?

1142. What areas does the group agree are the biggest success on the Service Lines project?

1143. Did the Service Lines project team have enough people to execute the Service Lines project plan?

1144. Did you do things well?

1145. Based on your Service Lines project communication management plan, what worked well?

1146. What was learned?

5.1 Procurement Audit: Service Lines

1147. Does the department evaluate and benchmark the performance of the procurement function/ unit against other comparable procurement functions/ units?

1148. Is the procurement Service Lines project efficiently managed?

1149. Are internal control mechanisms performed before payments?

1150. Is a risk evaluation performed?

1151. Is each copy of the purchase order necessary?

1152. Do at least two people have custodial responsibilities for negotiable checks (one checking on the other)?

1153. Is there no evidence of unauthorized release of information or seemingly unnecessary contacts with bidders personnel during the evaluation and negotiation processes?

1154. Were any additional works or deliveries admissible without the need for a new procurement procedure?

1155. When performance conditions were detailed in the tender documentation, did the contracting authority verify if the tenders received met the already stated requirements?

1156. If the expert was allowed to submit a tender, was all the relevant information the expert had gained from his earlier involvement made available to the other bidders?

1157. Does the individual having check-signing responsibility review the use of the signature plates?

1158. Is there an effective risk management system continuously monitoring procurement risk?

1159. Were the tender documents comprehensive, transparent and non-discriminating?

1160. If an electronic auction or a dynamic purchasing system was used, did the tender documents specify details on access to information, electronic equipment used and connection specifications?

1161. Was the overall procurement done within a reasonable time?

1162. Does your organization use existing contracts where possible to avoid the cost of bidding?

1163. Does procurement staff have skills to procure complex or special items (i.e. IT)?

1164. Is the purchasing department facility laid out to facilitate interviews with salespersons?

1165. Are reports based on sound data available to the already stated responsible for monitoring the performance of contracts?

1166. Are regulations and protective measures in place to avoid corruption?

5.2 Contract Close-Out: Service Lines

1167. What is capture management?

1168. Was the contract type appropriate?

1169. Was the contract sufficiently clear so as not to result in numerous disputes and misunderstandings?

1170. How is the contracting office notified of the automatic contract close-out?

1171. Are the signers the authorized officials?

1172. Change in attitude or behavior?

1173. Was the contract complete without requiring numerous changes and revisions?

1174. Has each contract been audited to verify acceptance and delivery?

1175. Parties: Authorized?

1176. What happens to the recipient of services?

1177. Have all contracts been closed?

1178. Change in knowledge?

1179. Have all acceptance criteria been met prior to final payment to contractors?

1180. Have all contracts been completed?

1181. Have all contract records been included in the Service Lines project archives?

1182. Parties: who is involved?

1183. How/when used ?

1184. How does it work?

1185. Why Outsource?

1186. Change in circumstances?

5.3 Project or Phase Close-Out: Service Lines

1187. What could be done to improve the process?

1188. Have business partners been involved extensively, and what data was required for them?

1189. What process was planned for managing issues/ risks?

1190. Planned completion date?

1191. What are the mandatory communication needs for each stakeholder?

1192. Is the lesson based on actual Service Lines project experience rather than on independent research?

1193. What is a Risk?

1194. Can the lesson learned be replicated?

1195. Was the schedule met?

1196. Planned remaining costs?

1197. Which changes might a stakeholder be required to make as a result of the Service Lines project?

1198. What information did each stakeholder need to contribute to the Service Lines projects success?

1199. What information is each stakeholder group interested in?

1200. What are the informational communication needs for each stakeholder?

1201. When and how were information needs best met?

1202. Who is responsible for award close-out?

1203. What advantages do the an individual interview have over a group meeting, and vice-versa?

1204. What could have been improved?

1205. Does the lesson describe a function that would be done differently the next time?

5.4 Lessons Learned: Service Lines

1206. What regulatory regime controlled how your organization head and program manager directed your organization and Service Lines project?

1207. Who managed most of the communication within the Service Lines project?

1208. Would you spend your own time fixing this issue?

1209. Did the Service Lines project management methodology work?

1210. What is your working hypothesis, if you have one?

1211. How well do you feel the executives supported this Service Lines project?

1212. How much of your time was spent on other than this Service Lines project?

1213. Will the information remain current?

1214. How useful was your testing?

1215. How long did redeployment take?

1216. How effective were Service Lines project audits?

1217. How much communication is socially oriented?

1218. What needs to be done over or differently?

1219. What are the funding priorities for intelligence?

1220. How well did the scope of the Service Lines project match what was defined in the Service Lines project Proposal?

1221. Were quality procedures built into the Service Lines project?

1222. Overall, how effective was the performance of the Service Lines project Manager?

1223. Were the Service Lines project goals attained?

1224. How often do communications get lost?

1225. Are lessons learned documented?

Index

broken 62
budget   91, 100, 114, 139, 153, 173, 181, 207, 211, 229,
242, 247-248, 250
Budgeted   47, 190
budgets   26, 116, 152-154, 241-242
building   19, 94, 129, 149, 167, 243
burdensome   246
burn-in 249
business   1, 7, 11, 18, 20, 33, 48-49, 63, 69, 76, 82, 87, 105,
107, 110, 112, 116, 119-120, 122, 127-128, 140, 142, 181, 184, 190,
197, 202, 211, 213, 221, 241, 250, 258
button 11
buy-in 249
called 135
cannot163, 173
capability   130, 138
capable   7, 38
capacities   107
capacity   19, 79, 130, 237
capital 118
capitalize   239
capture   52, 99, 186, 256
captured   61, 81, 142, 155-156, 193, 208, 220
capturing   223
career 144, 191, 226
careers   114
carried 70, 213
caseload   229
categories   241
category   33
caused   1, 56
causes 45, 54-55, 58, 62, 69, 72, 95, 136, 152, 205, 241
causing   21
celebrate   83, 227
center 50
central 197, 223
centrally   85
certain 169, 195
Certified   212
chaired   8
challenge   7, 223
challenges   110, 193
champion   28

controls   23, 63, 71, 82, 85, 88, 92, 97, 99-101, 163, 205
convention   121
convey   1
convince   189
cooperate   179
Copyright   1
correct44, 90, 137-138
correction   153
corrective   95, 200
correspond   9, 11, 152
corruption   255
costing56
counting   121, 157
counts 121
course 42, 48, 244
covering   9, 99
covers 176
coworker   106
crashing   163
craziest   111
create 11, 27, 67, 108, 219
created   61, 94, 131, 200, 205, 216
creating   7, 45
creative   19
creativity   88
credible   179
crisis   26
criteria 2, 5, 9, 11, 30, 33, 38, 68, 80, 85, 91, 109, 112, 126, 144,
180, 182, 209-210, 256
CRITERION   2, 17, 28, 44, 58, 74, 90, 102
critical 35, 39, 42, 61, 88, 96-97, 113, 134, 138, 158, 169-170, 215,
223-224, 241
criticism   231
cross-sell   106
crucial 68, 162
crystal 13
Cultural   132
culture 32, 58, 191
cultures   229
current41, 44, 48, 65-66, 70, 75, 78, 100, 103-104, 106, 119, 142,
149, 164, 169, 176, 183, 187, 191, 193, 199-200, 207-208, 211, 229,
245, 260
currently   38, 112, 153, 211, 223, 230

question 12-13, 17, 28, 44, 58, 74, 90, 102, 118, 134, 187, 235
questions 7, 9, 12, 172, 225
quickly 12, 63-64, 71, 197
radically 68
rapidly 169
rather 118, 258
Rating 234
ratings 210
rational 190
rationale 223
reached 23
reaching 115
reactivate 106
readiness 39, 207
readings 100
realistic 23, 67, 122, 201, 215
reality 203
realize 51
realized 250
really 7, 22, 31, 138, 141, 190
reason 104, 114, 199
reasonable 76, 115, 155, 207-208, 254
reasonably 152
reasons 33, 185
reassess 207
re-assign 159
reassigned 181
rebuild 108
recasts 177
receipt 246
receive 9-10, 36, 49, 195
received 33, 193, 231, 253
receives 234
recently 11, 104
recipient 21, 256
recognize 2, 17-19, 23-24, 26-27, 79, 83, 87, 170
recognized 17-21, 23, 26-27, 62, 138
recognizes 24
recommend 103, 120, 146, 196, 232
record 187, 230
recorded 194
recording 1, 246

repair   175
repeat 213
rephrased   11
replace   47
replacing   140
replicated   258
Report 5-6, 83, 100, 139, 161, 217, 239, 247
reported   146, 186, 243
reporting   64, 91, 108, 140, 146, 154, 169, 199, 246
reports 49, 96, 131, 177, 193, 219, 226, 254
repository   155
represent   82, 181
reproduced   1
reputation   103
request   5, 141, 181-182, 209, 219-222
requested   1, 78, 221
Requests   219
require 29, 58, 68, 97, 153, 165, 199
required   19, 25, 31, 35-36, 38-39, 52, 71, 75-76, 78, 94, 132,
134, 140, 157, 159, 170, 186, 193, 198, 204, 211, 213, 230, 237,
258
requiring   131, 256
research   25, 108, 112, 226, 258
reserve 153
reserved   1
reside   84, 155, 178
Resistance   213-214
resolution   71, 78, 195
resolve 19, 26, 159, 227
resolved   173, 178, 197
resource   3-4, 110, 159, 165, 167-169, 176, 193, 208, 213,
217, 229
resources   2, 9, 21, 24, 37, 39-40, 45, 76, 94, 97, 110, 116,
122, 127, 132, 146, 157, 159, 163, 168, 170, 172-173, 180-181, 194,
201, 211, 215, 235, 237
respect   1
respond   134, 200, 229
responded   13
response   25-27, 93, 95, 98, 248
responses   84, 124, 209
responsive   172, 179
result   63, 80, 82, 146, 179, 194, 221, 256, 258
resulted   98